THE DIARY OF
Lying Lovers

ROSE VENTRESCA

WESTBOW
PRESS®
A DIVISION OF THOMAS NELSON
& ZONDERVAN

WestBow Press books may be ordered through booksellers or by contacting:

WestBow Press
A Division of Thomas Nelson & Zondervan
1663 Liberty Drive
Bloomington, IN 47403
www.westbowpress.com
1 (866) 928-1240

ISBN: 978-1-5127-0471-6 (sc)
ISBN: 978-1-5127-0473-0 (hc)
ISBN: 978-1-5127-0472-3 (e)

Library of Congress Control Number: 2015911708

Print information available on the last page.

WestBow Press rev. date: 07/27/2015

*People had suggested to my husband and me to write a book on all that we had gone through. I have felt badly for many years over some of these situations and didn't know how I could possibly put it out there for people to actually read. My true inspiration to write this story came from listening to the Christian radio station while driving one day. They were on the topic of turning bad things to good, negative experiences to positive, and it was then that something inside me said, **"Write that book! Go ahead – you need to do this."***

All of a sudden it just felt right, and to my surprise, I was excited to get home to start this project. I had to turn a negative few years into a positive, eye-opening book. I had to listen to God's voice.

CHAPTER 1

I was always under the impression that there are two types of people in this world, good people and bad. There is one thing that both types of people do have in common, though. It's that not everything we do will be good-hearted. Doesn't that put us all in the same boat then, and not in a category of good person or bad person?

We can be defined as a person, as a human, but not as good or bad. Our actions, whether they be good, mean, mediocre, sweet, helpful, etc., they are what we *do*, not who we *are*.

In the fall of 2005, I was sixteen years old. My mom's name is Misty and my dad's name is Emit. They broke up when I was in fifth grade, so I just lived with my mom, her boyfriend of just a couple years, my brothers and sisters. We moved to a place called Sunset Acres. I had so much fun living there. It's an old Military base with all of the old Military barracks and homes.

There were about twenty of us that would hang out from the time we got home from school until the time we had to go in for bed. In between those times, we would only go in if we had to use the bathroom or for dinner. On some days we would be so cold, but it didn't matter. We always found something to do.

I met a boy named Rocky after we moved into Sunset Acres. Rocky was not hard to fall for. He was sweet, funny, caring, and I thought he was so incredibly good looking. Rocky was seventeen and he was just getting ready to leave five months later for basic training; he had joined the United States Army.

When Rocky introduced me to his parents for the first time, I thought they were wonderful, just so down to earth and very easy to talk to. Rocky's parents and I got along really well; they were very kind to me from the start. Rocky's mom's name is Renza and his dad's name is Dom.

Rocky and his neighbor, Brayden, would come to my bus stop almost every day to wait for my bus. Brayden was tall and looked about eighteen, but was only twelve years old. Rocky was like a big brother to Brayden. On one particular day when I got back from school, we walked to Rocky's house and his mother, Renza, was standing outside.

"We're going to rob a bank," she said very nonchalantly to Rocky as we got close, then she laughed and said that she was joking.

Rocky faked a confused laugh. He looked at me and rolled his eyes.

About an hour later, Renza asked that everyone go home. She said that she needed to talk to Rocky and tonight wasn't a good night for everyone to hang out because she also needed Rocky's help with some things, so I went home.

Rocky stopped by unexpectedly an hour and a half or so after I went home. I found out, much to my surprise, that the woman wasn't kidding about robbing a bank. Rocky said that Renza approached him about robbing a bank after I left their house; he said that he was completely taken aback. I hadn't taken her seriously for one second when she had mentioned it earlier. I laughed with her at the time, just assuming it was an inside joke or something.

They were in jeopardy of losing their home, something that was hidden from Rocky up until that point. Renza told him that she didn't care if she wound up homeless, but she would not let that happen to her husband, especially because he had MS and needed to be appropriately cared for. She told Rocky that nobody would give her a loan because of her credit scores and when Rocky told her that he would just get a job to help out until he left for the army, she told him that it would not help because he would not receive his first paycheck for two weeks, and by that time they would owe even more money.

I didn't really know what to think about this when Rocky told me. I was kind of in a tough spot. I was falling in love with him and we hadn't been together long, so I was going to just mind my business. Renza had only known me for a short period of time; I couldn't believe she would say that in front of me, especially after realizing that she indeed meant it. I never got the impression that she was the bank robbing type, or even capable of thinking such a thing.

Rocky was angry that the situation about the house hadn't been brought to his attention sooner, when he could have easily gone out and found a job to help with the bills. When they moved to Sunset Acres, he didn't look for work because he didn't have a car of his own and he was only there until he had to leave for basic training.

"I'm not doing it! I'm her son! Why would she put me in this spot? I have so much ahead of me that this could mess up!"

I knew that Dom needed a lot of help during the day; Renza took good care of him. I felt badly for them and I wished I had the money to give them. Rocky was sort of down in the dumps because he didn't know how he had never realized their situation before. I'm sure his mom just didn't want him to have to worry, so she kept quiet about it as long as she could.

Two weeks after that, my mother and I drove to the laundromat to wash our clothes. As we walked in, we noticed that Renza was inside standing at a dryer. She was just getting ready to fold her clean clothes when she noticed that I was there.

"Hi Rose! How are you guys?" she asked. "Rocky should be here any minute."

I was excited when she said that he was going to be there soon, because we were still in that early stage when being boyfriend/girlfriend is still new and exciting. I still had all the butterflies in the stomach, always waiting for him to call or text. About five minutes after we put our clothes into the wash, Rocky walked in and whispered for me to come outside with him. What he told me next stunned me.

"I robbed the bank," he whispered.

I had so many thoughts running through my head. I didn't think that it would ever really happen. So stupid! He could have gotten caught and gone to jail! We both got in the car so we could talk more. Rocky showed me the money that was hidden in the center console. When he opened it,

I could not believe my eyes! I was looking at the most money I had ever seen at one time, stuffed into a center console like an over-packed clothes drawer that took force to shut.

"My mom sat me down yesterday and talked to me. I'm leaving soon, and how will I get through basic training not knowing if my parents are being kicked out, not knowing if they are sitting comfortably in their own living room? Especially my father! I looked into getting a loan, but I can't because I am only seventeen. I told her no at first, Rose. I swear I did, but later something made me change my mind. I don't know what, but something told me to do it." I thought to myself, *yeah – your mom.*

"Was it because she's your mom? Because she isn't a stranger or just a friend, but your mom, and when your mom thinks something is okay, it's usually because it is? Because we trust our moms, and the more she tells you to do something, the more it becomes a possibility."

"I know right from wrong, though, and I chose wrong," Rocky said.

The sad part was that I could understand why he ended up doing it. I didn't particularly agree with it at all, but I understood. He was more susceptible because he was a teenage boy being asked to do this by his mom.

I began to picture one of my parents asking something like that of me, and I could see how I would be more easily persuaded by my mom or dad. I don't know if I would actually agree to do it, but I could see being torn. I was very sad that he did it, though.

Both of our mothers were still in the laundromat, so we got out of the car to go inside. When we got out, he looked at me.

"If I get caught, it's what I deserve."

Inside of my head, I had to agree with him, but I wouldn't say that to him and I wouldn't want that. Rocky locked up the car and as we were walking into the laundromat, behind us we heard a woman's voice.

"Sir, is that your car? Does that car belong to you?"

My heart was in my stomach. I could hear the nervousness in the tone of Rocky's two-worded response.

"Yes, ma'am," he said very hesitantly.

She then asked him to please move his car because he was parked in the company van's parking spot. We both just looked at each other and I could see his instant relief. He immediately moved the car for her. That little episode was incredibly nerve wracking.

There really wasn't as much money as I had thought I saw. I guess being stuffed into a tiny space made it appear to be more than it actually was. It was still a good amount though, close to $2,000, which would seem like a nice little chunk of change to most, but unfortunately it wasn't close to being enough for Rocky's mom and dad. They owed almost $3,000 on the house and still had to pay bills and buy groceries. I was surprised that the landlord that they rent from hadn't evicted them before it reached such a high balance, although she was finally starting to threaten eviction.

Renza put that money toward what was owed, and it bought her a little bit of time to try to come up with the rest. Rocky was leaving for the army soon and was always worrying about what was going to happen after he left. He was so worried that they would lose their home and there was nothing he could do.

I think Rocky felt a great deal of disappointment as well. He had a hard time talking about the fact that he had robbed a bank—he couldn't believe it, and he would immediately change the subject every single time that it came up. I think he was also bothered by the fact that the robbery didn't even get him enough money to fix the problems. He felt like he did it all for nothing. He felt like a failure both for actually doing it *and* for not doing it right.

He was mad at himself for reason on top of reason. This was just a seventeen–year-old boy with the weight of the world on his shoulders! I kept hoping that he would lighten up soon, because it was over and done with and he couldn't take it back. It was something he was going to have to live with for the rest of his life.

I was really starting to miss my funny, goofball boyfriend. I just wanted to have a good time again and enjoy our new relationship before he had to leave in just a few short months.

CHAPTER 2

It had been about a month since Rocky robbed that bank. Renza, Rocky, Brayden and I had to go to the reservation to get some cigarettes for Dom. After we got what we needed from the reservation, Renza stopped by her mom's house and ordered us all subs from this little pizzeria. Once we arrived at the pizzeria and got our food, we ate our subs outside in the parking lot.

It looked like Renza was thinking about something...she kept staring into nowhere. When we were all done, we got into the car and started driving home—so I thought. It turned out that Renza had other plans. She pulled into a Bank of America just around the corner. She found a parking spot and parked the vehicle, and I immediately started to wonder.

I sat in my seat quietly, praying we were not here to do anything other than legally withdraw or deposit some money, but I knew better. I started to feel sick and very nervous. I knew why we were there as soon as Rocky spoke to his mom.

"I didn't know this was your bank, mom...what are we parked here for? Are you going in?"

"Hold on a minute, Rocky. Just let me think."

I already knew what was going on. Renza looked back at Brayden.

"Do you have it in ya? Are you still up for it?" she asked him.

Brayden nodded his head. I watched Rocky's jaw drop. He looked at Brayden and then at his mom. Brayden put on the Carhartt jacket, grabbed the note to give to the teller, and took Renza's phone so he could look down at it until it was his turn in line.

I watched Brayden walk into the bank and my stomach started turning. *I'm going to jail today,* I thought to myself.

"I didn't know that we were coming here. I do not want you here; I don't want you to be a part of this. I am so sorry," Rocky told me, putting his head down into his hands. "Mom, Rose can't be involved in this!" he said angrily.

Renza looked at me and said *"I'm sorry"* with her eyes. She looked like a river could start flowing down her cheeks at any minute. I felt like I was going to throw up, and I was very mad deep down for them taking me there.

Brayden was taking too long. It had already been ten minutes when Brayden finally came walking out. I don't know if it was because time seemed like we were in slow–mo, but he was not getting to the car very fast, and he had money sticking out of everywhere. Brayden was only twelve years old robbing a bank—that really saddened me.

When he got into the car, Renza quickly pulled out and got onto the road. Brayden was in the backseat with me. I just wanted to hug him and tell him that everything would be okay, although he did not seem to be troubled by anything. I was hurting for him because he just robbed a bank and we were still likely to get caught. Cops were flying past us and Brayden had his head ducked down.

Rocky looked like he had steam coming from his ears. I just wanted to get out of the car.

It took ten minutes to get back to Renza's. After we pulled into the drive way, I finally felt some relief because we had made it home without getting stopped. I felt sorry for the bank tellers. Not one of them deserved to feel like their safety was compromised while at work; how awful.

We went into the house and Renza started to count the money. I sat down on the couch, feeling really awful about what I had just been a part of. Rocky came and turned on the lamp before sitting down next to me. He started to play with my hair.

"I'm so sorry that you were involved in that."

Renza finished counting, and said that she had almost enough to save their house. At that time, she owed another $1,000 for the current month on top of the already unpaid balance. Brayden only got $2,700. She said that she had $4,700. She reminded us of her other bills and utilities that were soon to be shut off, and that Dom needed his prescriptions, too.

"How do you have $4,700 when Brayden only got under three grand?" I asked her. "I went and got $2,000 last week, but I messed up… I forgot to take back the note," she said.

All of a sudden Renza looked like she could burst into tears and began talking a mile a minute.

"Wait what am I doing? Have I lost my mind? I think I need to take this money back. Maybe we can take this money back!"

Rocky, Brayden and I sat there in silence staring at her as she began to pace back and forth and then lit a cigarette. Then she walked outside and we heard the car start up. Rocky said he'd be right back, but he came back into the house because she left before he could reach the drive way. She wasn't taking the money back because it was still in the house. It was as if she just realized that she was the mastermind behind three bank robberies.

She wasn't answering her cell phone, and Rocky was starting to get aggravated and worried. She came through the door twenty-five minutes later, with her eyes red and puffy from crying.

"I needed to be alone for a little while, I'm going to use the money I have toward what I intended, and then you all don't have to worry anymore. It's over."

CHAPTER 3

Two months went by. It was around mid-January. After the last bank that Brayden robbed, Renza made Rocky a promise that she would never do anything like that again; she would never take anything that wasn't hers ever again. This gave Rocky some relief. He was hoping that it wasn't temporary relief, because he just wanted all of that to be over for good.

I had moved in with Rocky and his parents in January because my mom's boyfriend, Sparky, had made living at home almost impossible for me. His name is Joel but his friends call him Sparky. My brothers and sisters still lived there, so I was sort of mad at myself for not sucking it up and staying with my siblings. I left them with that monster and it ate me up inside.

Sparky yelled and screamed at us all the time and was just completely awful to my mom. My eleven-year-old brother, Joshua, was the only one of us though, that he had ever tried to touch in a fit of rage. He seemed to have some sort of a vendetta against Joshua.

One time Sparky went after him, and my mom tried to get in the middle to keep him away from my brother. While Joshua was standing on his bed, he punched Sparky in the face while Sparky's arms were flying around my mother trying to get him. Joshua was so scared. He was a tough little guy, but had the biggest heart of gold. Sparky didn't mess with Joshua physically again after that.

I kept going to school because I completely loved everything about being in school. I loved all of my teachers and friends. Rocky got a job working at Kmart because even though Renza and Dom were almost out of the woods with their bills, he did not want money troubles to make his mother desperate enough to try another robbery while he was home, so he was paying the utilities.

I got a job, too. I worked at the mall, which was just a minute and a half drive right down the street from Rocky's job. I only planned on working there until the spring, when I would switch to my grandparents' ice cream parlour. It was only open in the warmer months, and my family all worked there.

Until things calmed down, I would sneak home and spend time with my brothers and sisters when my mom and her boyfriend would leave. After I moved in with Rocky, it was hard not seeing my mom and siblings on a regular basis. I was living just around the corner, only a one-minute walk away. It wasn't long, though, before things did start to calm down and my mom started having me over more and more. Soon after that, everything was back to normal. Those kids were my life. We'd been through so much together—too much! My little brother, baby Emmit, passed away of SIDS in 1997 and nothing has been the same ever since. My mom became depressed and couldn't be a mom at that time, and then my parents broke up. The pain of losing a child was just too much for them to bear.

On the night of my 5th grade chorus concert, my dad dropped me off to perform. I asked him if he was coming in to watch and he said no, that he was going hunting again for a few days. He gave me a big, long hug and I got out of the car. Unbeknownst to me at that time, he wasn't going hunting, he was moving out. I did notice though, that the back of his car was full of boxes.

I was sad as I got out of his car, because I just wanted someone to come and watch me sing. We went without heat a lot. My mom kept my grandparents away, so they couldn't help us yet because they were unaware of the extent of our living situation. When we would come home from school, my little twin sisters would be running around naked. Clothes actually became adhered to the basement floor. Later on when selling the house, the clothes actually had to be scraped off of the basement floor.

I felt helpless because I couldn't give my little brothers and sisters a happy life. I was the oldest. I felt obligated, but I felt useless because I didn't know how to be a mom that young. I was only in elementary school and I was trying, but failing. I didn't know how to cook. I couldn't work and I couldn't do laundry, but I could wash the floors!

My mom wasn't the mom that we used to know. She was hurting. She was in constant pain, and I didn't know if she would ever go back to being her old self again. Losing my brother was a shock, one that my parents couldn't handle. One moment we were a family and the next moment I was crying on the floor next to my bed every night after my brothers and sisters fell asleep.

My grandparents were my heroes. They soon began to catch on that something wasn't right, and my grandfather went to my school to talk to my counselor, whom I had confided in. She brought him up to speed a little. When he walked out of the school, he spotted a building for sale across the street and said that at that moment he decided he would buy that piece of property and try to turn our lives around. That's how Elizabeth's Ice Cream Shop came about. They did that for us so we could have somewhere to work and get our minds off of being at home, and also make a little money.

When I hit eighth grade my mom started getting better and did a complete turnaround. She started working, and smiling again, and was working on her appearance. People thought she was my sister and all the boys in my school liked her. I hated it. At least she was getting back to herself again, a caring mom. That's the long-story-short version on what my brothers, sisters and I went through. We really have been through a lot.

Meanwhile, at Rocky's house I began to notice that Renza was down all of the time. She had not been herself at all lately. I didn't know if she was upset because her youngest son was leaving soon, or because she was worried about their living situation, being unsure of what would happen. Maybe it was a combination of everything.

Renza and Dom had a room booked at the casino for the weekend coming up. Maybe it was just what she needed to clear her mind. Renza and Dom had a few free rooms stacked up from all their spending there which would easily explain how they got themselves in the situation they were in, in the first place. She liked to go to the casino whenever she could because she was convinced that she would get lucky. She didn't have much spare money at all, but she so badly wanted to turn her few dollars into thousands.

Everyone wants to win, but not everyone will win. I have personally only known two people to win a substantial amount of cash gambling. I have a lot of family who have been going to the casino for years, even way before I came along. Out of all of the people that I know, for only two people to only win big one time—and I am talking under $10,000—the odds were just not in her favor. Sometimes, though, our vision is cloudy because hope can alter what we see in front of us.

◆

I was excited when the weekend finally came. I was off from school for two days and Rocky's parents were spending the night at the casino. I loved whenever they would go for a night at the casino because we would invite one or two of our friends over (Brayden was usually one of the two we invited), order the 5-5-5 deal at Dominos, and we would watch movies all night in the living room! The living room was where Dom stayed all day until bedtime, so we'd have to watch TV in our own room. It was only on the nights when they left that we get to watch TV in the living room.

We bought a movie at Wal-Mart, and it ended up being so scary that I flipped the recliner over backwards. No idea how I managed that one, but I did! The next morning when we woke up, Rocky felt like riding to the reservation. Rocky and Brayden had motorized razor bikes; they were so much fun in the snow! I borrowed Brayden's so Rocky and I didn't have to ride on the same one. We bundled up, got on the bikes and took off.

It took about twenty minutes to get to the reservation on the razors. When we got there, we picked out some hot chocolate and usually got some Lunchables to eat. We always bought hot chocolate. We tried all the different kinds that we could find, like double Dutch chocolate, French vanilla, Milky Way, etc. That was our thing.

My cousin Bobby was home on leave for a month. Funny enough, Bobby was one of Rocky's best friends growing up. I could not believe that I'd never met Rocky before moving to Sunset Acres, especially since he was my cousin's good friend. I didn't know why Bobby was home on such a long leave, but we had a blast. Bobby had a party at his mom's house every Friday and Saturday for the four weekends in a row that he was home, and a couple of little get-togethers during the week. The time started going by way too fast because we were having so much fun!

Rocky's departure date to leave for Basic training was March 23rd of 2006. That date was getting closer and closer. We had a few weeks left together, but the time was flying by. He had signed up before we met, which probably was a good thing because maybe he wouldn't have left if that hadn't been the case, and I didn't want to hold him back from any dream he had.

I was proud of him and happy for him. It was a new chapter in his life, but I would miss him so much. I'd stand by him through anything. I would wait for him back home, and then follow him to any destination. I loved him.

CHAPTER 4

The morning of Thursday, March 23, 2006, had arrived. I woke up knowing that this was going to be the last time I'd wake up next to Rocky for a long time. On our last night together, we went for a walk by the train tracks and watched the trains go by. We liked to do that once in a while.

Sunset Acres just wasn't going to be the same without Rocky. He was being picked up by his recruiting Sergeant at three o'clock. I went with him to visit some family members so he could say goodbye. We stopped by the laundromat to do a couple loads of wash, which made us run a little late. By the time we arrived back home to meet Sergeant Webber, it was already past three o'clock. It was time for him to go.

The depth of my sadness was something that I am unable to put into words; for those feelings, there were no words. Rocky ran inside of the house to grab his bags and to hug and kiss his mom and dad. Then he came outside and we said our goodbyes and hugged so tight—and just like that, he was gone. It was hard for me to bite my tongue as he was leaving. I could feel myself wanting to say *please don't go, just stay with me,* but I knew I couldn't say that to him.

I knew I would be heartbroken when he left, but I was really devastated. I suddenly felt so tired and empty. I tried to hold my composure as I calmly walked into the house, nonchalantly smiled at his parents, and fought my tears until I got into the bedroom. I shut the door, walked over to the fish tank, sat down next to it and broke down. I cried until tears just wouldn't come anymore, but quietly so nobody would hear me.

I could hardly wait until the next morning so I could go watch Rocky be sworn in. He had to go to MEPS. He'd spend the rest of his day there and also sleep there for his last night in NY.

I went to bed alone that night, and it really hurt. I sat up writing him letters. I tried to sleep so I wouldn't feel the pain, but I was an emotional wreck. Who was I kidding, I couldn't sleep. The last 149 days of my life had been spent with him, and I was in love. My first real love was off to the army.

◆

The next morning came so slowly. I was so happy when 5 a.m. finally arrived. I got ready, and then Dom, Renza and I left the house, first stopping at the reservation for gas and coffee. On our twenty-minute ride to MEPS, I was happy, nervous, excited, anxious—and very sad. I was excited to see him, but sad because I knew I had to say goodbye again.

When we finally got there and walked in, I saw Rocky sitting down. We got to talk with him for a few minutes. As I stood there looking at him while he talked to his parents and me, I kept think how amazing he was, and how handsome, too.

Time flew and then it was his turn to get sworn in, along with a few other guys. They brought us into a little room with flags and other men in uniform. He was asked if he was joining of his own free will.

"Yes, sir!" Rocky replied.

The sergeant said some other words and asked one or two more questions, and then he was officially sworn in. It was beautiful. I was so happy to be there to watch and be part of this huge moment in Rocky's life. I had never been so proud of someone before.

When he was all done and we all walked out, his parents said goodbye to him and they walked out to wait in the car. They wanted to give us a few minutes alone. We stood outside while he smoked a cigarette. He had his arms around me the whole time and we just talked about how we would miss each other and how hopefully time would fly by.

He finished his cigarette, and it was time for him to go in. We hugged and kissed. I tried to be strong, and I was. I whispered "I just want to stay with you" before we were done hugging. I just didn't want that moment to end.

I walked back to the car, got in, and we left. I stared back at the place where we had stood saying goodbye until it was too far out of my sight to see anymore. We were on our way back home and I was sad again, feeling very empty and lonely. I wished things could go back to the way they were just a few days ago—us being together, not apart. But Rocky was on his way to Ft. Campbell, Kentucky, and I was on my way back home, alone. I knew that this was going to be absolutely hard.

When we arrived back home, I walked into my room and started crying again. I hadn't eaten since Rocky left the day before, but I didn't feel hungry. Renza opened the door unexpectedly twenty minutes later to try to get me to eat some toast with peanut butter and jelly. She found me sobbing. She told me that everything would be okay and asked me if I wanted to take a ride with her to the store. I felt a little better leaving the house and riding to the store with her, but when we got home, the reality of Rocky being gone smacked me in the face again.

My mom came a little while later and took me to get my eyebrows done. I cried the entire time. I had such a horrible headache by that evening from crying. My mom sent my brother and sisters to spend the night with me so I wouldn't be alone. My headache was so awful that I couldn't even open one of my eyes. Suddenly, Renza walked in carrying the phone. With a big smile on her face, she said I had a phone call.

I grabbed the phone.

"Hello…"

It was Rocky calling. The sound of his beautiful voice was like music to my ears. I was so happy, I couldn't stop smiling. He said that he was doing well. He said that basic was hard; he liked it, though, but it was only his first day being there. He said although he missed me, his parents and his dog Snickers, he was happy that he was there. We only got to talk for about three minutes and then he had to go, but that three minutes made me happy.

Renza took the phone after we hung up. I sat up in my bed with one hand over half of my face and one eye because my head still hurt so badly, but I was so happy.

"I have a migraine!" I yelled with a huge ear-to-ear smile.

Everyone laughed at me. It was the first time I had smiled since the last time I saw Rocky. I had cried so much that I had made a tall pile of tissues. My sisters and everyone else who saw it got a good kick out of it. My sisters made sure they snapped a couple of pictures of my "tissue mountain of tears," as they named it.

I was supposed to move out once Rocky left, but the night after Rocky called me, Renza told me that If I wanted to stay and continue living with them that they would really like that. All of my stuff was already packed, but I decided to stay. Honestly, I was happy that she asked me to stay because I really didn't want to leave them. The bedroom was the closest that I could feel to Rocky while he was gone. It had all of our belongings, and everything that he owned in his room served as little reminders of him. At that point, I really needed all of those little reminders, so it felt really good to know that I didn't have to leave.

CHAPTER 5

Finally, the countdown began—counting down the days until June 1st, Family Day, and June 2nd, Rocky's Basic Training Graduation. I could hardly wait. I was starting to feel a little bit better, but I had to wonder, *if I'm taking basic training so hard, how will I react when he gets deployed?* I realized I had to suck it up and use this time for me.

I kept going to school and I wanted to save money, so when spring hit, I started working for my grandparents again at the ice cream parlour. It's called Elizabeth's Ice Cream Parlor, named after my sister Elizabeth. It's only a seasonal business. We were getting it all ready to open back up for the spring and summer. I also started working out and running every day.

Rocky and I wrote to each other every day. I always looked forward to the mail; it was the most exciting feeling when there was a letter or card in the mailbox for me. The few times when there was no mail for me were such bummers, and same for Rocky. Twice I flattened out a cigarette and sent it in a card for him, but one time he almost got caught so I stopped.

His phone calls were becoming few and far between. I would get so bummed out if I missed any of his phone calls at home, but sometimes he'd catch me at work if he had enough time or if they would let him make a second call. In Basic training he only got to make ten phone calls, if that, and he couldn't really plan them—he had to make them when he could.

Renza began going to church with her mom and she loved it, but she felt like God was still mad at her for what she had done. I told her it doesn't work that way. I asked Renza if she was truly sorry for what she had done.

"With my whole heart, Rose. With everything in me I am so, so sorry," she said as her eyes flooded with tears.

"Then the Lord knows that and he forgives you, Renza. He is your father and loves you like any father loves his child, except his love is stronger – he believes in you and is proud of your remorse."

The day came when Renza and Dom got some bad news...we did have to move out of the house because they were behind again and the landlord wasn't being lenient anymore, which was quite understandable. Renza told me there was just no way that they could keep the house any longer.

They had risked everything for nothing because they had to leave anyway. Renza quickly found us a nice place to move to, though, only about five minutes down the road. Although it wasn't far, it still crossed the school district limits and I would have had to switch schools, so I chose to drop out instead. At the time, it seemed like the better thing to do. I just wanted to keep working and saving money.

Moving out of Sunset Acres was depressing because I had so many memories there with Rocky. I would miss that house a lot, but I did like the new place, too. There was a nice trail out back that we would take Snickers for walks on. I wrote Rocky and told him about our new room and he wrote back saying he that he couldn't wait to see it. He never did get to see it, though, because we got kicked out after only one month of living there.

It happened one morning while I had Emma with me (the little girl I used to babysit; she had slept over the night before). We woke up to a lot of noise. I looked out of my bedroom window and there were Renza, Dom & Snickers standing in the grass watching as some men threw all of our belongings outside. Then there was a pounding at my door, and a guy yelled at me to get out before he broke the door down.

He didn't even give me a chance to open it. I would have cooperated, but he scared Emma and made me so mad that I started yelling back at him to stop pounding at my door. I could hear another man come to my defense; he told the guy who was yelling at me to knock it off. He told him it wasn't my fault that this was happening.

I walked out of my room and went outside. Standing in the middle of the mess, all I could think was, *Why? Can't we catch one little break?*

We called some movers and they came with a moving truck. Renza and I helped them load everything. Now, anyone who knows me knows that I am completely terrified of bees. If there is a bee around, forget it—I'm running. I've hurt myself more running from bees than if I would have just let them sting me!

Anyway, it just so happened that one of the moving men was scared of them too. It was a hot day and there were a ton of bees around. We were all trying to load this truck, but the moving man and I were running from bee after bee. Renza and the moving man who was not afraid of bees kept laughing at us. It was nice to see Renza smile and laugh even for just a few minutes.

Not long after that, we found out why we were being thrown out. It wasn't due to violating any rules & regulations, or being late on rent. They had rented out the apartment to not only us but another couple by mistake and since the other couple were friends of the landlords, you can guess who won that. They moved into our place the very next day. We thought about fighting it, but we figured it wasn't worth the trouble. And quite frankly, after that happened, you couldn't pay us to move back there.

Renza and Dom got two motel rooms at this little place about six miles away, a little farther away than I wanted to be, but it was something. Rocky wasn't allowed to know what was going on because they didn't want him worrying while he was at basic. So Dom would cut the grass and do work around the place in exchange for our rooms, temporarily.

The motel was in the country, so it was quiet and peaceful. In back of the motel was a little building with a radio and a pool table. There were also benches behind the motel. Geese were always back there and loved to chase people – especially my brother, Joshua!

The only thing that I was worried about now was getting down to Fort Campbell to see Rocky for his Basic Training Graduation. That day would be one of the biggest days in his life. If he were to look out into the crowd and see that we weren't there, it would crush him. That's one special day when all soldiers need to know they have somebody there proudly cheering them on and proud.

CHAPTER

Going to Fort Campbell was going to be a real challenge. The truck was broken. We needed money to fix it, plus we needed money for gas and food and a place to stay while being down in Kentucky. I had some money saved for Rocky's graduation, and I told Renza. She had been worried we wouldn't get down there, so that took a small weight off of her shoulders, but we still had to come up with some more money. I asked my grandma to hold some money out of my check every week. If I made $200, I would hold onto about $20 and I'd give the rest to my grandma to hold.

Dom was excited to go see his boy at his graduation. Rocky had a great relationship with his parents. Rocky's sister, Brynn, was also in the army, as well as his brother, Brad. Brynn was coming home on leave for a visit the same week that we were going to see Rocky.

Brynn's first night in, we had a great time. She and Renza picked me up from work. They got some beer and green apple Smirnoff. Of course I had to sneak a little, but they didn't mind. I was a good kid. Dom and Renza threw together a huge bonfire and we had hotdogs. The owner of the motel came out to join us. It was a really fun night, the best time I'd had while Rocky was gone.

The next morning, it was back to work for me. I liked working a lot of hours, especially now that I needed to stack as much money as possible for this trip. I was working every available hour that there was.

At the end of May, we were just a few days away from Rocky's Graduation date. I had saved enough money for Renza to have the truck fixed and she also had new brakes put on. I was beyond excited once I realized that this was really happening. It was becoming so real! Brynn was still home and she had a few weeks left on leave so she was going to drive down with us. We weren't going to have to travel with the dog since Brayden said he wouldn't mind looking after him. So we would pick Brayden up and he could stay at the motel with the dog while we were gone.

The next three days went by so very slowly. I just wanted it to be May 31st so we could leave already. I slept at my grandparents' house the night before we left. I like to sleep there once in a while and spend time with them. I love them so much; they are so good to my siblings and me. I was always very close with my grandma and papa. My grandma is a sweet-hearted little Italian woman and my papa is a big Sicilian guy with a huge temper but a big heart to go along with it. They're the most wonderful people I have ever known.

◆

May 31st, 2006, finally arrived. It was finally the day we'd get to leave. We picked up some drinks and snacks for the drive. I gave Renza all of the money that I saved up, well almost all of it, I held on to $80 of it. When we got back to the motel after picking Brayden up to dog-sit, I gave him $40.00 since he was going to be stuck there for a few days. We left soon after I gave him the money.

I was ecstatic! It was such a great feeling to know that we were finally on our way and I would see Rocky soon! We drove for hours and hours. I slept for a bit now and then. When we finally arrived in Ft. Campbell, we spotted a Burger King and we drove in and parked there for a while. Brynn and I got out of the truck and went inside to use the bathroom and freshen up. There really was no need to hurry because we still had another couple of hours to go. I was too excited, though.

Being on the base was the most amazing thing to me. It was an entirely new experience because I had never stepped foot on a military base before. Soldiers were everywhere, walking down the streets, sitting in Burger King and riding past in Humvees. It was so awesome; it was definitely one of the coolest places I had ever seen.

Every time a Humvee came by, I thought that Rocky would be in it, but he wasn't in any of them. We hung out and waited for the time to pass. Renza and I were sitting on the grass in front of where we were parked and talked to Brynn and Dom while they sat in the truck.

After an hour and a half had slowly passed, it was finally time to head over to where Rocky was. I couldn't believe that we were finally there in Kentucky and that in just a short time, I would see my soldier.

My heart was beating so fast, but my breathing felt short. My smile was ear to ear, but my hands were shaking. My mind was racing a mile a minute, but my mouth couldn't find any words to speak. I just sat there quietly in the truck as we drove to where we needed to be. I had no idea what to do with myself because the butterflies were going wild in my stomach.

As we pulled up to the location and parked the truck, we all kind of just smiled at each other.

"Well, here we go! You guys all ready?" Dom asked, practically beaming.

We got out of the truck and walked over to where the rest of the families were. I was so nervous that even my shoulders were getting chills. We were right up front. It felt like we were waiting so long—two minutes felt like twelve. Then it began! Out came the sergeants with the soldiers following behind. My eyes were all over the place searching anxiously for my Rocky.

It's him! I screamed inside of my head. I was so excited that I had spotted Rocky's face. There he was, right in front of me. He was so different—good different. He looked wonderful, like a soldier.

I was not looking at the same kid who left for the army's Basic Training; I was looking at a man, a soldier. He looked so professional. Tears just flooded my eyes and chills rushed all through my body. All the soldiers moved like they were one. Everything was in sync, step for step. They were on point with every march, every turn. It was incredible! I was so immensely proud of him, and it was one of the most memorable moments I have ever experienced.

When the soldiers were all finished, they came to greet their families. When Rocky came over to us, I didn't know what to do. I had been preparing for this moment since he left, but I was so excited, I was freaking out inside.

He first hugged his parents. I remembered his mom saying that the soldiers aren't supposed to show any emotion so when Rocky looked at me and walked a couple steps over to get to me I gave him a quick hug and let go. It wasn't the hug that I had dreamt about, but I was just happy to be with him.

I know that Rocky wasn't expecting to see his sister there for his graduation and he was very happy to see her. It would have been really nice to have his brother there, too, but he was serving another deployment.

We were so excited that it was Family Day and we were going to be able to take Rocky for the rest of the night and have him sleep at the hotel with us—but unfortunately, bad news was given to all of the families. Family day was being revoked and the families only got about two and a half hours with their soldiers.

I thought to myself, *what kind of luck is this?* Oh, I was angry! We drove all this way and we can't get him for just one lousy night because they have to report back to their barracks by 1700 hours—it was so unfair!

I was completely and totally bummed when I first heard the news of family day being revoked. I had to try and suck it up, though, because at least he was with me in that moment, and for that I was grateful. I didn't want to spend the little bit of time that we had with him being bummed out about something that we could not change anyway. The sergeants didn't even bother explaining why Family Day had been revoked.

The five of us got into the truck and headed over to the PX. We had the camera out and Brynn took pictures of us in the truck. We were having so much fun on the drive to the PX. We were very happy to be together. Rocky was so excited to have us all there.

We got to the PX and Renza, Dom and Brynn got out to go inside. Rocky and I hung out for a few minutes before going in. We were talking and music was playing on the mp3 player. He was holding me and I felt so happy. He talked about how he and I one day would get married—it was quick! I don't even know if he realized what he was saying to me, but the fact that he was thinking about it meant so much to me. It was a wonderful moment. I'd have given anything to marry him right then and there. The sound of his voice to looking at his face was absolutely nothing short of perfect in my eyes.

Rocky and I got out of the truck and went into the PX to meet up with his family. He introduced me to some of his buddies that we ran into while shopping; it seemed like everyone had come to the PX. Rocky bought me some perfume that I loved and had been wanting so badly; it was called Amore. Before we left the PX, Renza bought cigarettes and Rocky got a haircut, which you could do right at the PX. After his haircut, we were off to grab a bite to eat before we had to bring him back. We had about another hour and fifteen minutes with him.

The next day was his graduation day and then Rocky was going to be on his way to AIT in Fort Lee, Virginia. AIT stands for Advanced Individual Training. I was going to try to enjoy the following couple of days as much as possible because I knew that very soon after, I would be back to not knowing when I would see Rocky again.

While we were driving, Brynn fell asleep and Rocky was talking a little bit to me about his plans for after AIT, his plans for when he got stationed. What he said excited me and gave me butterflies. He said that when he got stationed, we would go look for a nice place to live. I couldn't believe that I was being included in his plans. I probably should be a part of them, of course because we're a couple. Still, it was so nice to hear what he way saying. I was getting all excited for the future, our future together!

After grabbing some lunch, it was time to head back to the barracks. We got back a little earlier than we thought we would, so he had time to hang out with us. Other soldiers were hanging out with their families, too. Some of Rocky's buddies would walk up to talk to him and he'd introduce them to his parents and me. After a few minutes, Rocky's parents said that they needed to run to the store to grab a drink. There was a store nearby, just about five minutes away.

Rocky had twenty minutes until it was time for him to report back. After they drove off, Rocky realized that he left all of his stuff in the truck and he couldn't report without all of his gear, so he was hoping they'd hurry up. Renza called almost ten minutes later and said they were lost. Time was really starting to tick.

"What am I going to tell my sergeant?"

A few more minutes went by before Dom and Renza finally pulled up. Rocky hurried over to the truck and quickly grabbed his stuff out of the back. Then he hugged & kissed everyone.

"I'll see you soon, sweetie. I love you," he whispered in my ear as his arms were wrapped around me.

Rocky started walking toward the barracks, but after walking just a few feet, he ran back to me for one more hug and kiss. Then he ran and caught up with a couple of his buddies. I watched until he walked through the door, until I couldn't see him anymore. It reminded me of when we were leaving after his swearing in at MEPS before his basic training. It seemed that I was often watching him until I couldn't see him anymore.

CHAPTER 7

After searching for a hotel, we found our best bet was Holiday Inn. That was where we were going to stay for the night. It wasn't far from where Rocky was, not that I'd get to see him again, but I felt a little better knowing we were still close to him. Brynn and I shared a room. I knew that Rocky should have been there with us, but at least I would be seeing his face bright and early the next morning. At least I wasn't alone—I had Brynn with me. Brynn was always either on the phone or the computer with her new boyfriend. I could understand that, because I would have done the same with Rocky if I could.

That night Renza and I decided to walk across the street to get something to eat. There was an Arby's and we were super hungry. On our way across the street, Renza told me that she had a gut feeling that Rocky would not be stateside when he got stationed.

After we walked back to the hotel with everyone's food, I went in my room to eat with Brynn. She was still on the phone with her boyfriend.

"Brynn, you're going to get married to this guy," I said.

"Oh my goodness, no I'm not! That's not happening anytime soon!" Brynn said smiling and blushing.

"Well, I just better be there when you do get married!"

The rest of the night, we just hung out and watched TV. Well, the TV was on, but I thought about my love every second, and Brynn talked on her computer with her boyfriend.

Around 9:00, she told me that she was leaving.

"You're leaving to go...where?" I asked.

"Sorry, but Greg bought me a ticket to come spend the rest of my leave with him."

I was a little saddened that she was going to go. I absolutely did not want her to leave, but I completely understood because if Rocky bought me a ticket to go be with him, nothing could stop me from going. Still, I enjoyed her company so much, and I knew I would really miss her when she left.

4:00 am came rather quickly. The phone rang and woke me up; it was the front desk down in the lobby calling to wake Brynn up and tell her that her cab was waiting outside. Brynn threw herself together and grabbed all of her stuff. I gave her a hug and then she was out the door, just like that. A few hours later, around 7:00 am, it was time for the rest of us to collect all of our things and get out of there. We had to start heading to Rocky's graduation.

When we got to the graduation ceremony it was raining, so instead of sitting outside on the bleachers and watching the ceremony on the large field, everyone headed into the building. We found three seats next to each other and sat down. While we were waiting for the ceremony to begin, I pulled out my camera and made sure that it was ready to go.

After waiting twenty minutes, the sergeants came out. I looked over to see Dom & Renza both with the proudest look on their faces; I was sure if they looked toward me, they'd notice the same thing. We were so proud, and Rocky hadn't even walked out yet. This was their third time watching one of their children graduate from basic training. When we were in the truck on our way to Rocky's graduation, I got to hear about Brad and Brynn's graduation days too!

Finally, the soldiers started to march out all in line with the sergeants carrying and waving flags. I was looking around for Rocky, thinking it would be unlikely that I'd be able to spot him with what looked to be about 200 soldiers marching on that floor, but we actually found him! I felt so lucky to be there watching him! I was so glad and relieved we were there, because Rocky was able to look into the crowd and know we were there for him. That alone made every second of this trip worth it.

After the ceremony was over, we looked around for Rocky outside. It took almost twenty minutes to find him. When we saw each other, we walked up to each other with big smiles on our faces, I had butterflies in my stomach and I was so nervous, like we were going on our first date. It felt so good to have his arms wrapped around me when he hugged me. I took a couple of pictures of him with his parents. He looked so handsome in his Class A Uniform. His mom took a picture of me with him.

We only got about ten minutes with him. I dreaded having to do this again, but it was almost time for yet another goodbye. Time started whipping by and I didn't know how to make it slow down. Soon Rocky had just a couple of minutes left, and I could see in his eyes that he didn't want say goodbye or leave us either.

"Guys, I don't want to get your hopes up, but I might be allowed to take a short leave in the next month or so," he told us.

"Oh my goodness, really Rocky?" I said, unable to hide that my hopes were instantly a mile high.

Rocky hugged me laughing.

"Maybe, maybe, maybe, hopefully," Rocky said, looking at the bus he was about to get on with other soldiers who were also heading over to Fort Lee, Virginia.

The soldiers from the graduation were not all headed to the same destination; some went to other bases around the country. In Virginia, Rocky would begin his AIT course for 63B (Heavy Vehicle Mechanic). Rocky was great with cars. He loved to work on anything with an engine. When we had the Razor bikes, he would take one apart so it would be just in pieces and he would teach me all about each part's purpose, and we would put it back together. His mom told us that when he was little, he would take apart everything from clocks to mowers. His dad was proud of his talent with mechanics at such a young age—except when Rocky took apart something brand new. Those stories his parents told me always made me laugh.

Rocky looked at the three of us and spoke with his eyes. It was time for him to get on the bus and leave.

"I love you. I'm going to miss you so much," I said, making a valiant effort not to let tears well up in my eyes.

"I miss you already," he said as he hugged me. "I love you…I'll call you as soon as I get a phone."

I stepped back, smiled and felt one tear roll down my cheek as I watched him hug both of his parents and say goodbye. Then we started heading in one direction and he went in the other. As we were walking away, I turned my head and got in one more "love you" as I slowly waved goodbye. We stopped walking and turned around to watch Rocky board his bus. He looked back at us and gave us one last wave. Then we watched his bus drive away 'til we couldn't see it anymore.

CHAPTER 8

Our plans had changed, just a little. We weren't heading home just yet. We were heading to the base where Rocky's brother, Brad, was stationed. We had to make a vehicle switch. We were leaving the F250 there and taking the Camaro home. Brad would not be there when we arrived because he was deployed overseas. I loved the Camaro, but I was dreading being scrunched in the tiny backseat from there all the way back home.

After driving for a while, we stopped along the way and got something to eat. The truck began to act up a little just as we entered Tennessee, but we continued on our way down the thruway. Then the truck started shaking and the tires started to lock up. The next thing I knew, we were broken down on the side of the road! At that point I felt like we were never going to get back home.

A tow truck came and took the truck to Midas, the nearest shop. This was the very last thing that we could afford. The towing company gave us a ride to the nearest hotel. It seemed as if it was going to be a sad night with leaving Rocky, breaking down, and I was for sure going to miss my sister's birthday in two days—after I promised her I would be there to celebrate with her.

We got into our room and I watched a little TV. We talked about how crappy our luck was turning out to be. There was a restaurant downstairs inside of the hotel, so we went down there. It was a nice bar/restaurant.

Dom and Renza told me the story of how they met and stories of when they first started dating. They threw in a couple of crazy bar stories, too.

I ordered the chicken fingers, but Renza knew how much I loved baked potatoes, so she ordered me one of those, too. I told her not to because I was fine with chicken fingers and I didn't want to spend anything extra, but she wanted me to have my baked potato. She was always thoughtful like that, no matter what was going on. Under the circumstances, we were having a pretty good time with great conversation. We semi-forgot about our sadness and bad luck, and we were laughing together.

After dinner we walked back up to our room. I wasn't that tired, but I thought it might be a good idea to turn in early since it was the most comfort I would be getting for the remainder of the trip. The truck was supposed to be fixed by the next morning.

When we woke up, Dom called Midas and it didn't sound like things were going very well. Apparently, since they knew that we were stranded in Tennessee, they figured that they could pretend the truck was worse off than it actually was so they could charge us more. Little did these guys know that Dom was a mechanic before he stopped working, he knew everything that there was to know about vehicles. We took a cab over there. Dom and Renza got right in there with both barrels loaded, so to speak, the Midas guys got a bit nervous and were stuttering. It was kind of funny to watch.

"Well, how is this broke?" Dom kept asking them.

Stuttering attempts at explanations from the mechanics.

"But can't you explain how or why this needs to be replaced? It looks fine to me"

More stuttering attempts at explanations from the mechanics.

"Oh, well that's not what you said on the phone."

The mechanics said there had been a misunderstanding—they had confused two different trucks. There was only one truck there while we were there, but we gave them the benefit of the doubt because at that point all we wanted to do was pay them and get out of there. The three of us sat outside while we waited for them to get the truck ready for us to take. It was hot and something crawled up my pants and either bit or stung my leg! It hurt. I never even got to see what it was, I only felt it, but it left a huge mark! I used the shop's bathroom, and when I came out I found that the truck was ready to go. We hopped in and continued on our way to Georgia.

◆

It took us about five and a half hours to get to Brad's base; we had a smooth ride and no stops. Brad had left the keys in an envelope underneath the hood. We took our stuff out of the nice big F250 and stored it in the trunk of the little red Camaro. Oh, I felt scrunched already! Renza was driving, Dom had the passenger seat, and he had to move his seat upward to let me get in the backseat.

I was definitely going to miss my sister's birthday. If the truck hadn't broken down, we would probably have made good time. While we were driving along, Renza's phone got a call and it was Rocky! He made it to AIT and he got a cell phone. I was so happy! We all got to talk to him. The call ended much too soon, but Rocky and I kept texting back and forth. Every time the text alert sounded I got butterflies in my stomach. It was pretty exciting that he had his own phone now to use when he wanted. My phone didn't have roaming, so I just used Renza's. Renza said that whenever I say Rocky's name, I smile. I know, I feel over the moon when I hear his name, say his name, or think of him. My grandmother and mom say that my eyes light up, too, when I'm talking about him. I'm so in love, that's why! I love this love feeling!

We had been driving for about four hours when we decided to stop at a Wendy's, get something to eat and park for a while. We got in touch with mamma, Renza's mother, and asked her to wire us some money because we were so low on cash and definitely didn't have enough to make it all the way home. Fixing the truck just about wiped us out. All western unions were closed this late at night so she had to wait until around 6:00 in the morning to wire us anything. Until then, we stayed parked at Wendy's.

There were other families parked there to sleep as well. I was surprised. It was quiet; we were just relaxing in the car in the dark. Suddenly Renza's phone beeped. It was a text from a number that we didn't recognize.

"It's Greg, I married your daughter," the message read.

Just like that, short, blunt and straight to the point. This trip was getting crazier and crazier. If I remembered correctly, I had just told Brynn she was going to marry this guy two days before this. Renza called Brynn and confirmed that it was definitely true, she was a married gal!

I had to try to get some sleep. Throughout the night, I would wake up and my legs would be so sore. I was uncomfortable in every way, every position. I was scrunched and I kept thinking that sleeping on bricks might be more enjoyable. At 4:30 a.m., I woke up. After that, I was in and out of sleep until about 5:15, then I was totally awake. Dom and Renza were up, too. We got out, stretched, and even laid on the grass for a few minutes. It felt really good.

Wendy's was connected to a gas station, so we grabbed some coffee and gassed up, and then a little after 6:00 am, our money was ready to be picked up. We were back on the road by 6:40 with about thirteen hours of driving left before getting home. Eventually, Renza's phone battery died. We had no way of charging it, so we were without a phone. Not only could I not talk to my love, it was my sister's birthday and I wanted to tell her how sorry I was that I had to miss it.

We stopped at a store where there was a payphone and an outside wall outlet. Renza charged her phone and I tried to call my sister, Elizabeth. She wasn't around when I called, but I talked to my mom and she told me that they got Elizabeth a cell phone for her birthday and gave me the number. They hadn't given her phone to her yet; her party wasn't until 4:00. At 6:00 I decided to text Elizabeth.

"I love you so much, I wish I was there with you," I wrote.

"Oh umm ok," was her response.

Her answer said it all; she hated me for missing her birthday. I sent her another message.

"I just wanted to be there with you. We should have been back by now, but we had the craziest time. I can't wait to see you. I'm so sorry."

This time she responded, "Ok I don't know what's going on here."

She was obviously trying to be difficult, so I wrote one more message.

"Well I'm sorry, I love you."

She responded back with, "Who do you think this is?"

I finally realized I was texting Brayden the entire time and not my sister—oh man, that was humiliating! I decided to try that again, but this time I messaged the right number. My sister was not mad at me and never was; she just wanted us to get home safe. After reading to Renza and Dom all of the text messages mistakenly sent to Brayden, we got a good laugh, a much needed laugh. I really missed my sister! Actually, I missed all of my family. I was definitely starting to miss home.

We got back to the motel a little after 11:00 pm. We decided that we would unpack in the morning, because all we wanted to do was hurry in and get right into our beds.

CHAPTER 9

For the next week, Rocky and I were constantly texting and talking on the phone, which was a nice change. However, the letters stopped and over time I realized that I kind of missed our sweet long letters. I was not complaining, though, because nothing beat hearing his voice every day.

Rocky was granted leave shortly after arriving to Fort Lee. It was a three-day leave, but hey—it was better than nothing, and I couldn't wait. I was still working at the ice cream shop, trying to save up some money again. Working there was fun, especially working with my sister, Elizabeth. We always made work fun. I liked being there with my mom and grandma, too. I think I'm pretty lucky, getting paid to work with my family and always getting to have fun at work.

◆

The day that Rocky was coming home on his very first leave had finally arrived. We ran to the reservation to get some food, gas and cigarettes. I spent most of the afternoon cleaning my hotel room. I was not supposed to tell Rocky about the motel, but I knew he would find out eventually. Plus I didn't want to keep anything from him, so I told him after we got back from visiting him. Then he wouldn't arrive to an unpleasant surprise that might have put a damper on his first leave home;

he was prepared to see where we were staying. I must say, it was really not bad. We did enjoy it for the most part.

At 2:15, Renza pulled away in the Camaro to head over to the train station to pick Rocky up. I was getting ready as fast as I could, doing my hair and makeup. I left my door to the outside open because I was getting so nervous, I didn't know if I should go outside or stay inside and wait.

I decided the second I heard the Camaro pull back into the motel that I would stay in and let him hug and visit with his dad. I was so nervous that I stayed in the bathroom and kept working on my hair even though it was all done. I just couldn't figure out what to do with myself while I waited. The butterflies were going crazy in my stomach.

The way the bathroom was set up and the way the mirror was positioned, I was able to see from the bathroom into the main room. I heard a footstep, and another, and as I kept looking into the mirror I could see his face as he walked toward me. He came into the bathroom and I turned around and just smiled.

"Hi," he said.

"Hi," I said back.

We were both blushing and then he leaned down and gave me a kiss and a big, long hug. When we were through hugging I kept giggling and looking up at him and then downward and then up again. I was acting so shy, but I couldn't help it.

That night Rocky, Brayden and I went out back and played pool in the little rec house. The pool table cost money, so Rocky stuffed plastic pop bottles in each of the pockets so the balls would never fully go inside (I wouldn't recommend this because that is how they break). The next morning, we took Brayden home. Rocky stopped to visit some family. That night we ordered some pizza from Little Joes Pizzeria, and had some drinks.

The next day was going to be our last full day together before he left to go back to Virginia. Rocky wanted to take his parents apartment hunting when Renza got back from church, but she absolutely refused. She said she was not taking a penny from him and told Rocky that she loved it there. She was in the country and it was peaceful and beautiful, which it was, but I knew she was still beating herself up about the stolen money. She even said to me at one point on the car ride home from Georgia that she almost felt sick about taking my money. Even though she knew the money was specifically for that trip, she still didn't feel right. Rocky said that he was going to try to make another leave happen really soon. He was going back on the 19th, which was my mom's birthday, and also the day I was scheduled to take my road test.

Those three days had flown right by. Rocky was back at AIT and I passed my road test. Once again, I was trying to focus on saving some money and getting out of the motel and into an apartment. For us, it was not as easy as 1-2-3 to get into a place of our own. Of course I could go and live with my grandparents, but I didn't want to leave Dom and Renza because they took me in and always made sure that I never went without.

Renza couldn't work out of the home because she had to take care of Dom all of the time. She could run out and do errands and she could go to church with mamma, but she couldn't leave him for hours and hours at a time to work. And I didn't make too much money working at an ice cream shop. It was going to take a little time.

CHAPTER 10

Rocky was granted permission for another leave. It hadn't even been two weeks since he was home last—I could really get used to this! I often lay down in my bed at night and fantasized about our future together, about us getting engaged, married and then having a family. I pictured what our house would be like when I moved in with him. He told me that he would pay for me to go home every three months because I'm so close with my family.

Rocky tried to be home for my 17th birthday, but the scheduling didn't work out that way. This time when Rocky arrived home, it was another short leave, but just as exciting as the first time. We made sure to take a bunch of pictures this time. I got the cutest one of him in his uniform eating an ice cream cone, while his amazing big blue eyes were looking at the camera. His favorite flavor was "birthday bash."

On his second day home, we went to the mall. He said he had a little something planned for me to do there. Rocky took me into Ultra Diamond Jewelry to look at and try on engagement rings. I started shaking. I had never before felt so truly happy and excited. He was doing this to get a picture of the kind of rings that I like.

Happy and excited probably were understatements for how I felt. It was really indescribable. The feeling was incredible! I fell in love with a certain ring—it was a yellow-gold princess cut diamond. I couldn't wait to rock that ring around on my finger! I couldn't wait for him to propose so I could call him my fiancé!

Before we left the mall, we stopped at a photo booth and took a picture. He was giving me a kiss on the cheek in the picture and there was a heart around our faces. We also went to the movie theatre before going back home. We decided to see World Trade Center. It was a good movie—sad, but good. When the movie finished, people stood up from their seats, noticed Rocky in his uniform, walked over to him and shook his hand while thanking him. I was so happy to be able to witness that moment.

Back "home" at the motel, it was looking like we would be moving out sooner than we all thought, and not together. The owner of the motel didn't want to let us stay and barter two rooms for work around the property anymore.

Rocky was unhappy because when he was on his first leave and saw where we were living, he insisted on getting his parents out of there and paying for a place the first couple of months. Renza did not want to take his money. She refused to; she pretended that they just loved it at the motel. She said they loved the country (which they really did; they are country folks at heart). Nevertheless, Rocky was all set and ready to go out apartment hunting.

Renza wasn't having it. She called her stepmother, Natalie, down in Florida to see if she and Dom could stay there for a little bit. Natalie was excited that she called and that they were coming. So that was settled—Renza was not going to let Rocky pay for an apartment.

I started packing my stuff to go to my grandparents. I knew that my grandparents would be thrilled to have me; they had wanted me to be with them so badly from the start. Snickers couldn't go to Florida; she was a 14-year-old dog. I wanted her to come with me. Dom and Renza agreed to let me take her.

Later that night, Rocky and I went for a walk behind the motel. It was always so peaceful back there. We held hands and talked about so many things that night, mainly about the situation his parents were in. Rocky wanted to put them in their own place, but they refused to take his money and I knew why; I think he did too. Renza had said a few times after the last bank robbery that she would never take anything from anyone again, not even a gift. It didn't take a rocket scientist to know that she was refusing his money because she was regretful about the banks.

The next day was emotional for me. We were all packing our stuff into the little Camaro and we ran out of room, so Rocky was going to take me to my grandparents with Snickers and all of my stuff. Dom and Renza would stay behind at the motel and wait for Rocky to return and get the rest of their stuff. After that, they were going to take Rocky back to the train Station.

When it was time to head out the door, I realized that although living in a motel was not ideal, I was going to miss this place and my room there. I didn't have many exciting memories from this motel, but the ones I did have were among the best I'd ever had, like Rocky's first leave home, texting him all day, my first day back from his graduation while lying on my bed watching TV, even when Brynn was home and we had a big bonfire out back. Twenty-four hours ago I did not know that the next day would be my last day here.

When I walked outside and saw Dom standing next to their door, I burst into tears. I hugged him and told him that I loved him. He told me to stop crying and that they would be back soon.

"We love ya," Dom said laughing and hugging me. Dom had been like a father to me. Renza always called me Dom's little angel. I was still in tears saying goodbye to Renza, but she said almost the same things that Dom said—to stop crying, she loved me, and they wouldn't be gone long. I walked over to my room, took one last look inside, reached for the handle and shut the door.

◆

Believe it or not, the twenty-minute car ride to my grandparents was quiet. We were both sad, and the twenty-minute car ride felt like the time was cut in half. I just wanted to be with Rocky in that car as long as possible. When we pulled into the driveway at my grandparents' house, we got out with Snickers and Rocky brought all of my stuff into my room. When we went back outside, I was bawling like a baby. We kept hugging each other tight.

"Don't cry," he said. "Everything's going to be okay."

We said I love you to each other and kissed, and then I watched him walk to the Camaro. He looked back and said "I love you" one more time, got in and drove away. Once again, I watched him drive away until I couldn't see him anymore.

I went back into the house, into my room where Snickers was. I got down on the floor beside her and cried. Then my family's dog, Goldie, came in and laid with us like she knew I was upset. I could tell Snickers was sad, too—she was in a new home, her "brother" Rocky had just left her, her "mom" and "dad" were gone, and she was a really old dog. We had a private pity party as we lay on the floor together.

CHAPTER 11

It had been a couple of months since the last time I had seen Rocky, but we talked on the phone every day. He had a leave already planned that would put him home for several days.

Dom and Renza were still in Florida, but were getting ready to come back home. They were going to stay at mamma's place for a week or two, and then move into an apartment.

Snickers was not doing well. My papa wanted her to be put down so she wouldn't be suffering anymore. It was hard to even look at her. Her hips were visibly out of place and she had tumors on her. We wanted to hold off on putting her down until after Rocky got home so he could see her one last time, but even Renza asked us if we could go have her put down because she didn't deserve more time in pain. So my grandfather did. It was difficult to say goodbye to her.

Lately I had been hanging out a little at my mom's in Sunset. There's an in-ground pool for all of the people who lived there to swim in, and that was always fun. Everyone from Sunset was always at the pool when it was nice out. Elizabeth and I usually took our little sisters, Jaida and Julia, to the pool, and our little one-year-old brother, Casey. I was working just about every day. Not only did I like the paychecks, but it made the time go by quicker until I got to see my love.

October 1st, 2007, arrived and Rocky was on his way home on his third leave. We were a couple of weeks away from closing the ice cream shop for the season. We were staying open a little later that season.

My mom and I picked Rocky up from the airport. Rocky's mom said he could have the Camaro while he was home. They met us at the ice cream shop after we picked him up from the airport. I stayed at work so Rocky could go out with his parents and spend time with them. He came back about two hours later and picked me up. We went out and found the cutest little motel, close to his mamma's house. We stayed there for his entire leave. That leave went by much too fast. Since he was done with AIT, this would probably be his last leave for a while; when he got back, he would find out where he'd be going next.

On Rocky's second night home he took me to a super fancy restaurant that we had never been to before. After dinner he took me shopping at the mall and bought me a purse and some outfits as my belated birthday present. I had turned seventeen a few months ago and since he couldn't be around for it then, he told me at the time that he would make it up to me. He said that we would celebrate when he came home again, and that's what we did. I didn't bring it up to him and he still remembered!

After we were done, we went back to the hotel for the night. My favorite part of the nights when he was home was sitting on the bed while he'd tell me all about the army. I loved hearing all of his stories and about all of the new people he'd met. I hoped to be able to go to visit him out there soon, for once. I was hoping I could go after he received his orders. I had so much fun at Fort Campbell when he graduated, and couldn't wait to visit the next base that he'd be stationed at.

The very next night while we were sitting on the bed talking away, he told me to get ready. It was like I could almost see the lightbulb come on in his head! He told me not to ask any questions about where we were going or what was up.

We got into the car and drove until he pulled into Sunset Acres. It felt so weird to be there again with Rocky. We hadn't been in Sunset together since before he left for basic training. I missed it a lot, especially at that moment. We had some pretty great times there, and time was flying.

Rocky drove back to one of the farther streets, and as he parked the car, I knew why he had brought me there. We got out of the car and started heading for the train tracks. Walking to the train tracks definitely triggered some emotions. It felt like we had gone back in time to when we lived there. I felt so happy. I had spent most of my time missing him those days, so being together there now, especially in a place that meant something to us, was just so special.

We held hands and walked the tracks. We waited twenty-five minutes for the train to go by. We got so close that it was nerve wracking, but exhilarating as well! When the train passed us by, we turned around and walked back to the car. This was the first time after watching the train go by that we walked back to a car and not back to the house!

We went from there to Tim Horton's. We went inside and ordered our coffees and sat inside for an hour. I could have stayed out all night with him; I didn't want the night to end. When tomorrow came, it would be that much sooner that he'd have to leave me again.

When the night was just about over and we were back at the hotel, Rocky fell asleep first. I laid next to him and stared at him, kissed his forehead a few times and touched his sweet face. In a few more days, he wouldn't be sleeping next to me and I'd be missing him again. I knew it wouldn't be like that forever, but it felt like a lifetime waiting for our time to be together, living together again. Nothing else could make me feel the same way that being with him did. He made me feel like I was on cloud nine. Even after being together for almost a year, I still couldn't believe he was mine and I was his!

After four days of being home, Rocky was on his way back to Fort Lee, Virginia. He was all finished with AIT, so he was going back just to wait for his orders. Although he wouldn't receive his orders for a couple more days, we were pretty sure that he would be going over to Ranger School with Brad.

The following day, Rocky got the word that he was definitely going to Ranger School, so that was good news. I headed over to mamma's house to have some coffee with her, Dom and Renza. My favorite part of the day was having coffee with them every morning. When I got there, we each got a cup of coffee and went downstairs and sat outside to drink it since the weather was so nice.

Dom and Renza's plan originally was that when they got an apartment, I would go with them. However, it was a just one-bedroom, and I was pretty content at my grandparents' house. I loved being with my grandma and papa.

Dom and Renza's new apartment was across the street from the house Rocky grew up in. Their old house had been knocked down, so I never did see it, but Rocky would take me to the property all the time because the big barn was still up and they had a huge pond that is still there, too. I'd seen pictures of the house, and they talked about it often.

I applied for a job working at a little Italian restaurant; I was hired right on the spot. It wasn't bad—to my surprise, I did enjoy working there and I was making new friends, too. I even got a raise my second week there. Work was becoming so much fun, I didn't mind being there at all.

I went with Renza to confession where she confessed all that she had done to the priest. She told me she hadn't felt that good in a long time. She actually left there feeling like God had truly forgiven her. She said that she told God she wanted her kids to be proud of her and she wanted to be proud of herself too. She said that she was tired of thinking about what she did and cringing at the thought of it.

"I wish I had the same mind then that I do now; I would have never have done that!" Renza told me, and I knew it was true.

Renza being anything less than a good person deep down never crossed my mind, because she was a nice person regardless of what she did in her past. Renza didn't just say she was sorry for what she had done, but she wore her feelings on her sleeve, and her true feelings showed in her actions. I really felt that she should forgive herself. It was very obvious that Renza couldn't believe she ever did any of that. Renza even wanted to somehow find out who the bank tellers were that were working on those days and send them gift cards to a restaurant or something; she wanted to make it up to them in the worst way.

Rocky was on his way to Ranger school in Georgia and I wanted to do something sweet for him, so I went to the store and bought cookie dough to bake him cookies to send down. I baked a lot of cookies, and bought a nice little container to send them in. I didn't even have an address to send them to yet, but I made them anyway. By the next morning, he had sent me the address. I got everything together and, surprisingly enough, Sparky, my mom's boyfriend, offered to take me to the post office. It took only two days for Rocky to receive my package. He was so surprised!

"All of the guys here are enjoying the cookies that you sent!" he told me, laughing.

CHAPTER 12

On October 15th, 2006, Rocky was sent to be stationed at Fort Jackson, South Carolina. He failed the test for Ranger School; he was out late the night before and wasn't on top of things like he should have been. Ranger school is intense. It has been called the "toughest combat course in the world." It's oriented toward small-unit tactics. Sometimes we must fail in order to later succeed. To know how badly failing feels will help us fight to avoid feeling that again.

I had no idea when I would get to see Rocky next. He seemed to like it in South Carolina and he was with some of his buddies who also didn't pass Ranger School. Rocky was in the Airborne unit—he jumped out of planes and he absolutely loved it.

October 25th had finally arrived—it was our one-year anniversary. I was so excited for this day, even though we couldn't be together. We only got to talk to each other for just a little bit during the day because he had to work and then I had to work, but he did bring up marriage and how he would like us to start planning a wedding for some time around September. I was thrilled! It was not the proposal I had always dreamed about, but I did not care one bit. I couldn't have been happier.

After we closed up at work around 10:00 p.m., or 2200 hours (hey, I use military time, too, since Rocky's joined the army), I went outside with some co-workers to wait for our rides. I called Rocky and he answered, but sounded down. I wished him "happy anniversary." I could hear my coworkers saying, "Aww!" Rocky and I got off of the phone quickly; he must've just been tired.

The next day I went over to Dom and Renza's and hung out with them for a little bit. After I left, I called Rocky and he sounded a lot better; he was in a good mood. I asked him what he was doing and he said driving around with a couple of buddies, Gaeler and Smith. They all go by last names in the army. We talked for twenty minutes and then we got off the phone. He was driving his buddy Gaeler's car, which I thought was odd but I wasn't even going to ask.

Over the next couple of weeks, Rocky and I did not communicate much. He was out in the field a lot. One afternoon, I come in from walking to the store and I noticed a call on the house phone's caller ID. I noticed it was a South Carolina number and I quickly recognized the last name of Gaeler. I figured this must be Rocky's buddy. Only one problem, "his" first name was Morgan.

I thought to myself, *you know, maybe the cell phone is in his buddy's mom's name*, so I decided to call it. I dialed *67 in front of my number to block it. It rang and it was a girl's voice who answered the phone. I hung up. My heart was pounding; I was shaking and sweaty. I instantly called Rocky to find out who this girl was. Rocky answered the phone.

"Why are you pranking Gaeler and calling her names?"

"I did call her to see if a girl would pick up the phone, but I never said anything—I was speechless when I heard her voice! I did nothing but hang up."

"Well, Gaeler told me all of the things you said to her."

It looked like this "Gaeler" was just trying to cause trouble between Rocky and me, and get us into a fight. I couldn't believe my ears, though. It sounded like he was trusting her over me, and I truly hadn't said a word to her. Rocky then went on to say that she was his friend. Maybe he was right, why can't he have friends that are girls? But thinking back on the day when he was driving Gaeler's car, why was he driving her car anyway, and why was she trying to get him to turn against me?

◆

Two weeks had gone by since Rocky called me from Gaeler's phone. Rocky and I were barely talking at all, and when we did, there was tension and it felt like he didn't want to talk to me. I cried a lot to him, trying to tell him how I felt about us drifting apart, but we would just end up fighting. I felt absolutely horrible inside. It felt like we were going to break up.

I knew something was wrong, but I couldn't picture him really cheating on me. I was still doing a lot of wedding planning and having so much fun with it, but it would have been perfect if we were actually getting along. My only happy time lately was doing wedding-related things.

One day before I left for work, Rocky called me and we talked for a few minutes. Rocky had to go out and buy a cheap pre-paid cell phone because he was about to go over his minutes on his regular phone and his minutes automatically reloaded every 15th of the month. That other cell phone started ringing in the background so he told me to hold on while he answered his other phone.

It was Gaeler, and the sound of his voice while he was talking to her was very disturbing because he was so sweet with her and it stung when he told her that he would call her back in a little bit, and then before they hung up I heard him thank her for helping him with the TV. It was hurtful!

Rocky got back on the phone with me with a normal voice, not sweet like he was with her. I told him how it hurt me to hear how nicely he spoke with her and that I really didn't want him hanging around her anymore, but he told me that for now the wedding was off because I was acting crazy and if I didn't change soon, we were over.

Maybe it was me, or maybe he was just trying to convince himself that I was the problem. I had no idea anymore. I headed to work a little bit early and sat in the break room in tears, feeling so alone and not knowing what he was doing. A girl named Angela, who I usually don't talk to, came over to me.

"Are you okay?"

"Yes..."

"Rose, are you having Man problems?"

"No, it's just family stuff," I lied, too embarrassed to tell her that my fiancé wasn't in love with me anymore.

I had to do something to get my mind off of Rocky. I started hanging out with some old girlfriends, Bridget, Coley and Kara. It's nice to have girlfriends, especially when things aren't going so well in your life. I also got to see another old girlfriend, Crysten, which was nice. I also started talking to my friend Joe again. No matter how many friends you have, it doesn't fully take the pain away, but I was giving it my best shot.

My friend Bridget was dating a guy named Trave, who I hadn't met yet. Bridget, Kara and I went over to his place. We drank beer, watched the movie "Fight Club," and listened to music. I had a good time, although my grandparents thought that I was over at my friend Kaylee's. I hated lying to them, but I was just not feeling myself.

The next night, I was at home hanging out in the TV room—I usually stayed in the TV room because my room didn't have a TV and the TV room had a Futon couch; I sometimes slept in there, too.

I called Rocky and asked him what he was doing. He said that he was sitting in the car with Gaeler and another buddy of his. I was annoyed but I wasn't going to start because we were already on thin ice with each other. He seemed to have absolutely no interest in talking to me.

I finally had enough and told him that I'd let him go and to have a good night. Before hanging up, I said "I love you"—no response from him whatsoever. I was starting to get mad.

"You can't tell me you love me back?"

"Well, I'm going to get off the phone now," was all he answered.

"No, don't you hang up…you won't tell me that you love me in front of *her*! How can you be doing this to me?"

I gave him another chance to tell me he loved me back but he didn't.

"I'm done, we are through," I said, and I hung up.

Rocky sent me a text message saying, "How could you say those words to me? I would have never have said those words to you." *Well*, I thought to myself, *you're breaking me. I'm truly broken and you did that to me.*

I did not message him back, but as hurt as I was, I did not want it to be over for good. I was hoping somehow that we would get back together, but as hard as it was, I would not talk to him first. If we got back together, it would be because he wanted me back.

Rocky called me a couple of days later while I was at work and I let it go to voicemail. He left a message saying that he needed to get in contact with his parents because he got into a little car accident, but he was fine—just damage to the door. He could have called him mom's phone. I think that he just wanted an excuse to call me.

Over the next couple of days, I was getting private calls and when I would answer, nobody would speak. I could hear a little breathing, though. You know how you get a feeling and you just know? I knew those private calls were Rocky listening to my voice.

From the first ring of the very first private call, before I even answered, I could feel that it was Rocky calling me. If he missed me so badly, then why was he doing what he was doing to me? How many sixteen-year-olds would wait for their boyfriend of five months while he went and pursued a career in the military?

♦

Thanksgiving was just a couple of days away. Rocky had not called me and I had not called him. It was not easy to resist calling him, so when I wanted to call him and I felt like I almost couldn't fight it, I'd call my friend, Joe, instead. I even kind of "flirted" with him over the phone, and I felt bad because I did not have an ounce of feeling for this guy, but it helped me to not call Rocky. What I was doing to Joe was mean and I knew that, but my heart was really starting to shrink at this point.

The next night, my mom and I decided to head over to Renza's to visit them. It was going on 7:00 p.m. We brought over a pan that Renza needed, too. When I got there, Renza said that she had a feeling Rocky might surprise us and come home for Thanksgiving. I was so excited to hear that. Then she said to me, "I just have this gut feeling."

I started to think that she knew something I didn't know and she just wasn't telling me. Renza and Dom felt really bad about our break-up. I was worried, because I had thought I was going to have them in my life forever. I loved them. If Rocky and I were over, was my relationship with Dom and Renza over, too? We had been through so much together.

I had to use the bathroom. When I was walking to it, I noticed that their bedroom door was closed. That door was never closed, it was always open. Was Rocky hiding in their room to surprise me? That had to be it!

When I came out of the bathroom, I walked back into the kitchen, but I made sure to talk real loud to my mother and Renza. I laughed every second that I could find something to laugh about, because I wanted him to hear every word out of my mouth and hear that I was happy and that I was okay, to get him thinking. I hoped that while he sat in that room that the sound of my voice would make him melt. I wanted it to be hard for him to hide from me in there because he would want to come out.

After almost an hour, right before my mom and I were leaving, he still hadn't come out. I was beginning to think that maybe he was actually hiding from me rather than surprising me. We left and my mom took me back to my grandparents' house. I knew that if Rocky was home, I would know for sure tomorrow because I was spending Thanksgiving with my family and then heading over to Renza's to have dinner with their family.

CHAPTER 13

It was Thanksgiving Day and we were expecting the family to start arriving around 2:00 p.m. We usually started eating around three. I always helped my grandma get the house ready and I always try to help her with dinner, but she likes to do all of that herself. She is an amazing cook.

We always have a lot of people visit for the holidays: my grandparents, my mom, and Sparky; my siblings – Nico, Elizabeth, Joshua, Jaida, Julia, and Cash; my aunt Krista, Uncle Landon, and their four kids – Tony, Kari, Xander and Little Landon; my great grandmother Lucia, my uncle John Scott, and my great aunts Margherita and Carmella; plus myself. Sometimes my dad would come by, too, and we loved it when he did because we always missed him!

My plan originally was to eat with my family and then go over to Renza's, but I was too anxious to get there. Since I was done with helping my grandma around the house, I headed out to Renza's. Anyway, dinner was a little earlier there than at my grandma's this year, so it worked out fine.

I walked into Renza's at about ten to one and mamma, Renza's brother Jet, his wife Shelly and their daughter Alyssa were all there already. Renza's other brother, Joseph wasn't going to be there until later on, but this was my first time meeting Jet, Shelly and Alyssa, they're really nice people and

Alyssa was adorable! I had met Renza's brother Joseph a few times before, and he's wonderful, too.

I was very nervous because I knew any minute Rocky was going to walk out and surprise me. I just wondered if everybody was in on this surprise, or if he would be surprising them, too. After I got finished chatting and saying hello to everybody, I excused myself so I could use the bathroom. I did not really need to go to the bathroom; I just wanted to see if Rocky was waiting for me to find him, because I had already been there for ten minutes.

As I approached the bathroom, my heart was beating faster. The hallway didn't go straight back—once you got to the bathroom, you could turn left and walk into the bedroom, but you couldn't see the bedroom until you reached the bathroom. As I walked slowly into the bathroom, I turned my head to the left and I couldn't believe my eyes. The door was wide open and Rocky was not in there!

I went into the bathroom after staring into their room for a few seconds. What a let-down, but I knew I had let myself down because I should never have gotten my hopes up anyway. I sat in the bathroom on the side of the bathtub for a couple of minutes. I had thought today was going to be very different from what it was turning out to really be. I sat there and stared at the floor with my legs crossed and my head settled on my hand, with my elbow digging into my thigh.

Well, it was time to pick myself up and hold my composure, because I couldn't let them all see me down. I walked out and headed into the kitchen with everybody. We were all talking and laughing and, surprisingly, I did begin to have a good time! After a little bit, I started to feel less upset. Dinner was going to be ready in another fifteen minutes or so.

As we were sitting there talking away after everyone joined in at the table, the conversation topic shifted to Rocky and then they all decided that they were going to use the house phone to call him so everybody could talk to him. At that moment, I wasn't sure who all knew about my situation with Rocky other than Renza. Jet dialed his number. It rang but there was no answer so each one of them got on the phone and left a quick little message saying basically the same thing, "Happy Thanksgiving," and that they loved and missed him.

When it was little Alyssa's turn, she was so cute telling him how much she missed him with her little voice; she was about 5½ years old. When Alyssa was done, Jet grabbed the phone and turned to me.

"You want to say something, too?"

"Oh no, no, no…that's okay."

Dinner was ready, so we said grace and ate. The food was good. Renza's a really good cook. When we were all done, Alyssa went into the living room and drew me a couple of pictures. When she was finished, she, Dom, Jet and I walked across the street to the pond on the old property that Dom and Renza used to own. We were throwing rocks into the pond and walking around. Given the circumstances and the situation that my relationship was in, I was enjoying myself fairly well, but I was ready to walk back to the house. I couldn't wait to go and see my own family.

When I returned home, everybody was eating. I said hello to everyone as I walked in. I gave everybody a hug and a kiss on the cheeks while wishing them Happy Thanksgiving. In Italian families, you kiss both cheeks, not just one.

I started to feel a little sad. I couldn't wrap my head around the fact that Rocky and I weren't okay. I sat down thinking more about what was on my mind than what was on my plate. As I sat there eating my mashed potatoes, I realized that Rocky and I were no longer together. He was not my boyfriend and I wasn't his girlfriend any longer. I also realized that there was probably a good chance that he had made that other girl his girlfriend by now.

I couldn't eat anymore. I went into the kitchen and snuck a can of my papa's beer and went to my room. I drank the beer as tears rolled down my face. Rocky did not wish me a Happy Thanksgiving today, which was a good indication that he was happy, having fun, and not thinking about me.

A couple of minutes and a half can of beer later, my cell phone rang and "Private Call" read across the screen. I ignored it and kept drinking. It started to ring again. Instantly, I was not sad anymore, instead I was a little excited and felt more at ease because my gut told me that this was Rocky calling. I was also hoping that maybe he would speak this time because I decided to answer it.

Sadly, I said "hello" several times but got no answer. I finally just hung up, making sure to sound happy as could be. I did not want to give away the fact that I knew it was Rocky calling, or let him know that I was upset. After I hung up, there was no phone call back. I decided to go back out with everyone and spend some time with my family, especially my great grandmother and aunts before they left.

CHAPTER 14

Two days had passed since Thanksgiving and I still had not heard from Rocky. Today was day number seven since we broke up. I refused to let myself call him or fight to get him back, although that was what I really wanted to do. I was also afraid of what he'd say to me. I didn't want to hear words that would break my heart.

It was hard not to call him, but I thought it was better that way. Plus, he knew how much I loved him and right now, I doubted that he loved me at all. I knew if I called him and the phone call went well, or even if we got back together, I would always remember that he never came for me.

We were having a nice morning and papa had just finished making a huge breakfast for me. Usually all the grandchildren were here on the weekends, but this morning it was just me. I was sure they would start coming over one by one as the day went on.

My grandparents' house had always been the place to be for all of my cousins, siblings and me. My papa had owned many businesses—currently two successful businesses. My grandma worked for a big company called VIP. My grandparents had a lot of money. Their house was always nice and cozy for all of the grandchildren, because we all had very little growing up. My grandparents always made sure that at least when we were at their house, we felt happy.

I was starting to feel something I had never felt inside before. Anger wasn't even the word for it. I wanted Rocky to feel the pain that I felt. I was starting to feel hatred toward him. I had trusted him with every ounce of my being, and all he was doing was jabbing a knife in my back and twisting. This would only have happened to me; maybe I was too nice. I was sick of being nice.

♦

At 11:00 a.m., my grandma was cleaning the house and I was vacuuming for her. After I vacuumed every room in the whole house, I went into my room to turn my radio down. We had been listening to music while cleaning. I checked the time on my phone, and was hit with a shock. *Oh my goodness, I missed three calls from Rocky!* He hadn't left any voicemails. I didn't know what to do.

Should call him back or not? I had not been expecting to miss calls from him! In a way, I was relieved that I hadn't heard my cell phone ring and that he kept calling me; that part felt good. As I was still holding my phone with these thoughts racing through my head, my phone started ringing in my hand. It was Rocky!

I was freaking out inside, but I hit the answer button, put the phone up to my ear and said hello.

"Hi…I've been calling you…"

"I was cleaning with my grandma and I didn't hear the phone," I told him, keeping my voice happy but neutral.

We spent about another forty-five minutes on the phone. Happiness took over and all my angry and hurt feelings went away. Rocky told me that he didn't want us to end, and that he wanted us to work things out. He said that we would take it slow and not worry about getting married right now. That part kind of stung, but we could get back there again. I could handle that for now.

I wanted to bring up the other girl. I wanted to tell him she needed to be out of the picture, and they could not be friends at all because all that she did was poison our relationship…but I decided to let him do all the talking. I knew if I brought her up, it could start something. I just hoped he would end his friendship with her on his own. It seemed as if we were all good again, and when he had to go, he told me how much he loved me. I ran out to the living room and told my grandma the good news. She was so happy for me.

I realized as the next couple of days went by, that I was not so sure that things were really back to normal between Rocky and me. Before, I would call him whenever I wanted. Now I felt awkward calling him, and he didn't call me as much either. I only texted him when he sent me a text message first.

This was just all wrong. I felt I just needed to deal with it and work toward the relationship we once had, but I didn't know how to get that back. I wished I could speak my mind to him, but I was always too nervous about getting into an argument, so I just let everything go. But inside, I worried and beat myself up because I felt like I was not good enough. I just felt like he didn't love me as much as before.

Rocky called me while I was babysitting at my mom's house. He had just gotten a new truck and wanted to make sure that I had gotten the pictures. In the pictures he sent me, he was parked next to a streetlight because it was dark out and the streetlight lit up the picture a bit. I could see the truck pretty well. It was a red 1998 GMC Sierra. This was another reason I was still unsure of his feelings for me, because normally he would have been on the phone with me all the way to the dealer, but I didn't even know he was buying a truck until after he bought it. He said he was sitting in his truck outside of the barracks waiting to go in. It was almost a quarter after nine, and he said once he went in he was going to go to bed. He was being really sweet to me.

I told Rocky to go in and I'd stay on the phone with him, but he told me he couldn't be on the phone after he went in, which I thought was a little weird because he has talked to me plenty of times while he was in the barracks. We got off of the phone and I was happy because it went so well.

We had laughed on the phone and he said sweet things to me, but at the same time I couldn't help but think that he was not waiting outside of his barracks. I didn't question him; I was avoiding causing an argument at all cost because I didn't want to lose him and I still had hope that we would get what we had back.

I wished I could be like other girls who say what they want when they want, and have their boyfriends wrapped around their fingers. I was starting to think that I needed to change some things about myself, but I don't know what. *There must be something wrong with me*, I was starting to think.

I felt like I was starting to dislike myself. I just wanted Rocky to love me. I had always been so good to him, but being good to him was getting me nowhere fast. I wished I were different. I wished I didn't care, but maybe I could teach myself to not care. Easier said than done.

Over the next couple of weeks, Rocky and I hadn't fought at all, but that's because we'd barely talked either. He and I talked on the phone maybe once every couple of days, and sent a few text messages back and forth a day.

Bridget called and said that she and Kara were going over to Trave's and that I was in some definite need of some time out. I walked over to Bridget's house and Trave was pulling up as I walked up, so I set my stuff in his truck and ran in to let Bridget know that we were there. She wasn't done getting ready when I walked in, so it was about five to ten minutes before we walked outside to leave. On our way out, Bridget's phone rang. She answered it.

"Yeah, she's right here," she told someone and handed me the phone.

I took the phone, figuring it was my grandparents calling to check on me since my phone was with my stuff in Trave's truck, but it was Rocky!

"Rose, I've been calling you—where've you been? How come you haven't been answering your phone? I was getting worried…"

I was so happy to hear from him. We talked for a few minutes.

"Bridget, Kara and I are going to Trave's. We're in his truck."

"Really? Let me talk to Trave," Rocky demanded, so I put Trave on.

"Hey, Trave, you better be driving safe with Rose in the car! There better not be any alcohol in your system while you're driving with them!"

"No, man that would absolutely never happen. You don't have to worry."

Trave gave the phone back to me.

"Listen, Rose, even though I'm far away, if you have any problems, I want you to call me, okay?"

"Sure, Rocky. Okay."

When we hung up, I had so many thoughts running through my head. I was ecstatic. That phone call showed me that he did care for me. I had crazy butterflies. He hadn't called me at night in so long, and since our problems started he usually didn't call more than once, but tonight he must have really missed me. I grabbed my phone out of my bag and saw that I had three missed called from him. The rest of the way to Trave's house, we blasted the radio and jammed out to Three Days Grace. Nothing could ruin my mood because this was the happiest I had been in about three months.

The next night I slept at Bridget's house. She had a really nice finished basement so that is where we spent most of our time and where we would sleep. We ordered some food and we talked, laughed, and just hung out. After a while, my phone started to ring. It was Rocky! Two nights in a row he had called me—I couldn't believe it! He said he was hanging out with a couple of his buddies. We talked for almost an hour and a half. For a little while, we were both on speaker phone so his buddies, he, Bridget and I were all talking and it was awesome. We had so much fun talking together. I thought Rocky and I were getting closer again. I loved him so much.

Two days later, my cell phone rang around 8 o'clock p.m.; it was Rocky calling me. I answered the phone.

"Hello?"

"So what are you doing tomorrow?" he asked.

Instantly I knew something was up.

"Um, nothing," I said in a confused tone.

Rocky laughed.

"Do you want to come to South Carolina?"

He told me to get online and look up bus tickets, and that we would put it on his debit card. After looking at bus tickets, I wanted to check out pricing on plane tickets because the bus tickets were more expensive that what I had thought. I ended up finding a cheaper plane ticket that was $153.00 round trip, which was not a bad price at all and better than any bus prices. I called Rocky and we put it on his card.

I couldn't even believe this was happening. When I got up that morning, I did not think by the end of the night I'd have booked a flight to go visit Rocky. My flight left in two days, on December 17th. I'd come back January 3rd.

I was going to spend Christmas and New Years with him! There was only one thing that I was not looking forward to, and that was not being with my grandparents, siblings, parents and the rest of my family for the holidays. I would miss them, but I was looking forward to being with Rocky, too. This was unexpected to say the least, but this was the perfect opportunity to get our relationship back to the way it was before.

The next day came and it was my dad's birthday. I called him early that morning to tell him that I would be leaving for South Carolina the following day. After talking to my dad, I called my papa. He was not too happy about me going, but I expected that and still it went over with my papa better than I expected. My papa was usually pretty strict and very over-protective, but that's what you get when you're the granddaughter of a Ventresca. I wouldn't have had it any other way though.

Later that morning, my mom and little brother took me to Big Lots and Wal-Mart to get some things for my trip. After shopping, they took me home and I got all of my stuff packed, then I sat on the bed and started thinking and getting a little nervous. I had only been on an airplane once before.

As happy was I felt that morning, I kept thinking about everything Rocky had put me through in the last few months and I started to feel a little bit of anger and sadness. That was the last thing I should have been thinking about, because it really looked like everything was changing for the better and going back to normal. Still, Rocky had broken my heart and I was still trying to glue the pieces back together. I was worried about Rocky hurting me again, and I was hurt that I had to worry about him hurting me.

When I looked back at the start of our relationship, and when he left for the service, when we went to his basic graduation, when he would come home on leave and when he took me to look at engagement rings…I wondered why we had to go through such a hard time, because we had something so special. I wondered if maybe I wasn't good enough. I wondered if I was madly in love with someone who wasn't in love with me anymore.

Now that I was going to South Carolina, maybe I would get to have some words with Morgan. I should have been so happy, but I was feeling sad inside thinking about all of this. That was kind of out of character for me. I was normally a very happy girl, but the last three months had taken a toll on me and made me feel things I wasn't used to feeling.

My papa and mom were taking me to the airport in the morning. I had to be there by 6:00 a.m. By the time I was ready to go to sleep, I was feeling a lot better, plus I had been able to talk to Rocky—but just for a few minutes. He thought it was a good idea that we cut the call short so when we saw each other the next day, we would have more to talk about. I didn't think we would run out of things to talk about, but it was cute the way he said it on the phone, so of course I went along with it. Falling asleep was hard because I was so excited about the next morning. I could hardly wait. I was excited and nervous at the same time.

My mom woke me up the next morning. I was exhausted; I really did not want to get up. I felt like a zombie. I just wanted to close my eyes and go back to sleep because I had barely slept a wink. I finally got up, brushed my teeth, said goodbye to my grandma, grabbed my bags and met my papa out in the car.

My papa surprised me and gave me $300.00 to travel with. My dad told him to give me an extra hundred from him and my dad would drop off the money later that day to pay him back so I had $400.00. I knew I would be getting money to travel with, but I didn't think I would get that much!

I got to the airport at exactly the time that I was supposed to arrive. We got some Tim Horton's on our way there. Their coffee was so good. It was hard to say goodbye to my mom and my papa, especially around the holidays. I was just hoping that I wouldn't regret this trip. I hoped it would fix everything between Rocky and me and rekindle our relationship, because Rocky had my heart. I knew we would soon see what was going to happen. It was time to board the plane.

I missed my papa and my mom already, and I was starting to get super nervous! I brought a few magazines with me to help pass the time. It was not a long flight, only about two and a half hours.

At just about 11:00 a.m., the plane started its descent. I couldn't get over the fact that I was in South Carolina; it was my first time. We finally landed on the ground and were moving toward the gates where we get off once the plane came to a stop. It wouldn't be much longer until I was finally with Rocky!

I had a winter coat on because when I left home it was cold (but a bit warmer than our usual winters). It looked like I wouldn't need my coat in

South Carolina; it was really sunny outside. As I sat in the plane waiting to get off, I was so excited about Rocky waiting for me inside.

I was hoping the fact that he had flown me down meant that he had cut all ties with Morgan Gaeler. What if he hadn't though? I would not be okay at all with that. I realized that was something I probably should have found out before I came. I couldn't believe I didn't think of it beforehand, but I was supposed to be enjoying myself, not getting myself all worked up over all of this again.

I started to calm down a little. I told myself, *it's not worth it—she is not worth it*. She would get her karma, I was sure of it, for what she did to me. I completely held Rocky accountable, too, for putting me in such an unfortunate situation, but the fact of the matter is, it's only natural to blame the other party more.

Finally it was time to get off of the plane. I grabbed my luggage and looked around for Rocky; I didn't see him anywhere. I had a Cricket cell phone carrier, so I could only use my cell phone locally at home because they hadn't expanded their towers yet. I had to search for a payphone to call him.

I found a payphone right around the corner I anxiously dialed his phone number. He answered and said he just got there because the drive took an hour and he had to find the airport. I told Rocky where I was and he said that he would be right there.

After we hung up, I waited for about four or five minutes. During that time I kept fixing my hair, checking my makeup, and checking my hair some more. Finally, there he was! I could see him at a distance walking my way. I stayed where I was and let him walk to me. He had a friend with him.

Rocky looked so cute walking toward me. He had a light shirt on with some dark green cargo pants and he was wearing a hat. I'd never seen him in person with a hat on other than his beret. We had exchanged picture messages once in a while—he had sent some recently with him wearing a hat, but seeing him in person walking toward me, he looked so good… he was gorgeous!

He walked up to me and the butterflies in my stomach started going crazy. He hugged me, gave me a kiss, grabbed my bags and we headed for the door. He was blushing and I could sense that he was so nervous.

He looked at me often as we were walking out to the truck and we would both laugh. He was genuinely excited that I was there and he didn't even have to say it.

On our way out of the airport, Rocky introduced me to his buddy, Calvin Roudacush—but they call him Rouda. Again, they go by last names in the military. Rouda was really nice. I finally got to see Rocky's new truck. When we got to the truck, I hopped into the back seat, while Rouda got in the front seat with Rocky. Rocky's truck was even nicer than the pictures.

We talked about my flight and about life back home. We were laughing and the conversation was good. I couldn't help myself for what I was about to do, honestly I just could not. I asked Rocky to let me use his cell phone so I could call my papa to let him know that I made it safe and sound. I was eyeing his cell phone from the second that I noticed it sitting in his cup holder. I had to wonder what was in it, what messages or when the last phone call between Rocky and Gaeler took place.

Rocky handed me his cell phone and as I pretended to dial, I went into recent calls and saw Gaeler's name so I clicked on it and let it ring three times. After it rang the three times, I hung up the phone and pretended that my papa didn't answer the phone, and then I hurried up and deleted the outgoing call out of his recent calls list. It worked like a charm because not even two seconds later the phone started ringing in my hands and it was her.

"Who's calling?" Rocky asked.

"Uh, Morgan Gaeler," I answered in a confused tone.

Rocky said not to answer it, but of course I had to.

"Hello?"

"Hello," she answered. "Who's this?"

"Morgan, this is Rose. Please leave Rocky alone and never contact him again…"

Rocky was laughing and trying to grab the phone from me. Before it could go any further, I just let him have the phone and he hung up on her.

It felt so unbelievably good to let her know that I was there and with Rocky. I realized that three months ago I would never have done anything like that, but at least I was finally starting to stick up for myself. I must have been through a lot of hurt in the last couple of months for me to do something like that, and on top of it, to feel good about it!

"I'm so sorry," Rocky looked at me through the rearview mirror and said with just his lips, not his voice.

He seemed sincere; he looked almost sad. It made me feel really good and at that moment I had a good feeling that everything was going to work out with Rocky and me. I was starting to believe he really did love me even though he had hurt me. Every couple has to go thru a rocky path, and maybe that had been ours.

The three of us were hungry, so we decided to stop and get something to eat. We stopped at CiCi's pizza buffet and ate there. I still couldn't believe that I was really there with Rocky in South Carolina! I loved it there—it was so warm, I had to ditch the winter coat the second that I walked out of the airport. As we left CiCi's, I still just couldn't believe the weather, it was so beautiful.

CHAPTER

At the barracks, I went into Rocky's room with him. Rouda went into his own room. The barracks were like apartment buildings. There were nine doors on the ground floor and nine on the top floor. Through each door was a kitchen, a bathroom and three bedrooms. They were so much nicer than how I pictured them to be. Rocky had one roommate. He said his roommate was nice, and he did seem to be nice, but he seemed to keep to himself and played video games the majority of his spare time.

I was finally in Rocky's room. It was like a dream. I still couldn't believe I was there with him. I was so happy, and everything felt almost back to normal. When I say almost back to normal, I do mean only almost. It's not easy to explain; the best way I can put it is that everything was wonderful, we were head over heels for each other, but the two of us right now compared to the two of us every time that he came home on leave were a little bit different.

Rocky used to be overly caring and super gentle from the way he looked at me to the way he spoke with me. It wasn't that he wasn't caring with me now, because he was. It just wasn't to the extent that it used to be. It was as if something was on his mind that was holding him back from giving all of himself. He was being wonderful to me, but something was missing now compared to what we had before.

We laid down on his bed and talked and cuddled. We started to kiss. I had been longing for this moment for quite some time, not knowing a couple of weeks ago if I would ever be in his arms again. I just wanted that moment to last forever. There was no better feeling than being in his arms.

I happened to look over at his desk and I noticed his many pictures taped up. I'd seen them before because he had sent me pictures of his room. When he sent me the photographs of his room, there were pictures taped up of me, his parents, his mamma, Snickers, and all of my family. There was one little difference now—every picture of me was gone.

I decided to let it go and not bring it up. If he was hiding me he should have at least put my pictures back up before I arrived, there is no way I wouldn't notice that. Maybe it was too hard for him to look at me while we were broken up. I just hoped that it wasn't because he was hiding my pictures because she had been in his room.

I kept hearing something in his closet, and I wondered what it was. I forgot he had gotten a pet chinchilla. I didn't know what in the world possessed him to go and buy a chinchilla. I guess it was cute that he had a little pet.

At eight o'clock, we still hadn't eaten, so we figured we would head out to get some food and also head on over to Wal-Mart after. Before we walked out of the barracks, he grabbed my arm to pull me toward him.

"Thank you for coming here. I didn't think you would. I didn't deserve another chance, but if you can't tell, just know I do love you and I think we're meant for each other," he said, looking into my eyes.

I smiled at him. He smiled back, and we walked outside. What he said gave me chills, I loved him so much. Rouda ended up coming with us because he also wanted to go to Wal-Mart. We ate at Sonic first, and the food was delicious.

After that, we went to Wal-Mart. I picked up some things that I needed like razors, shampoo, deodorant, etc. I bought Rocky some things, too. I also grabbed a CD that I wanted to check out, a band called Hinder, because both of the songs I had heard by them were pretty good. The lead singer, Austin Winkler, has a phenomenal voice. Rouda grabbed the same CD too. My first night in South Carolina was a success. I was so happy to be there.

◆

Rocky left early in the morning for PT. I was actually not allowed to stay in the barracks overnight or be there without Rocky, so we had to be careful to not get caught. If a sergeant found me, I was not really sure what would happen, but I know we would get in some kind of trouble. I wouldn't even use the bathroom while Rocky was out. I would just plan to sit in his room until he came back. Sergeants could walk into anybody's place in the barracks at any time, and the last thing I wanted to do was get caught by one of them.

After a while, I started looking around in Rocky's room. I couldn't help it, I felt like being a little nosey. I opened up his desk drawers… it looked like nothing but some important papers. I walked over to his nightstand and opened the top drawer…again, nothing. I quickly opened the bottom drawer, figuring it would be empty, too.

To my surprise, there before my eyes was a cell phone. I already knew that this must have been the cell phone he had to go out and buy when he went over his minutes. I quickly looked for the power button, and my heart raced because I didn't know what I was going to find on this cell, what messages I might see.

It turned on and it went to the home screen. I went into messages and there were messages between Rocky and Gaeler. One good sign to me was the fact that he had her in his cell phone as Gaeler, her last name, because I felt like if it was serious between them, he would keep her saved into his phone by her first name. I opened up the conversation. There were only about four or five messages. She sounded like she was upset with him.

"Where are you do u want to go with me"

She sent one shortly after; he didn't respond.

"Whatever I'll just go by myself then bye"

The next message was sent by him.

"What's your problem and I'm busy today"

I put the phone back. If they were just friends, why was she getting irritated with him like he was her boyfriend? Why would she get irritated that he didn't respond to her faster? This just didn't make any sense to me.

I didn't know why I put myself through that. I should never have looked for anything. I knew I was going to find something, I could just feel it. Should I bring it up to him or not was the question. I thought I'd keep this to myself so Rocky wouldn't wonder why I was snooping around through his room. Plus, the messages were from about a month ago.

I grabbed my suitcase to look for something to wear. I took out a pair of jeans and a nice shirt. I opened his closet up so I could stick my suitcase in there to get it out of the way. As I set my suitcase inside, I noticed an orange shirt hanging up—it looked like a girl's shirt. I quickly pulled it toward me and took a closer look.

It was definitely a woman's shirt with a V–neck. As much as I was trying my best to believe nothing ever happened between the two of them, it was getting really hard to keep telling myself that now. I didn't know whether to leave, to confront him, or let it be. Maybe the shirt was from a while ago too—maybe he forgot about it being in here. I didn't know if I could let this one go. This one really stung.

I leaned against the wall and slowly dropped down to the floor, and as I sat there a teardrop fell from my face to the floor. I looked down and saw a little tiny ripped piece of paper. In Rocky's writing he wrote his initials, and below his initials there was a heart and below the heart was my initials. My teardrop fell right into the heart. How did such a hurtful finding turn into a moment that was almost beautiful?

When Rocky came home from PT we started getting ready to go out. I couldn't take it any longer—I decided to let him know about the shirt that I found in his closet.

"Why is there a girl's shirt hanging in your closet, Rocky?"

"There are no girls' shirts in there," he said as he went over to the closet and opened it up. "Show me!"

I grabbed the orange shirt from the hanger.

"Here! Here is that girl's shirt!"

Rocky looked at me.

"Oh, this shirt? This shirt is mine!"

"I don't think so."

"Listen, Tarill and I bought girls' shirts and wore them around for Halloween."

I gave him that *"yeah, right"* look. That couldn't be true, it just couldn't. Did he think that I was born yesterday? He couldn't possibly expect me to believe that. Still, I told him I'd give him the benefit of the doubt. I wish I had more strength. The least he could do was be honest with me.

Would we ever get the relationship we once had back? I really didn't know now, except when I thought about the future and us being married, I saw us just the way we were before. I guess anything's possible. I love him so much, why couldn't it be easier?

We went to Sonic for dinner again. I could never, ever get tired of eating there. They had the best chicken sandwiches that I'd ever tried. After dinner, Rocky asked me if I wanted to go the movies, and I said sure. I still was not happy about the shirt, but I wasn't mad at him anymore. I usually can't stay mad at him long anyway. I wished I could, but my heart was still a little sad.

After the movies, we went back to the barracks and went to bed. Rocky had to be up early again for formation and PT.

CHAPTER 16

I was just getting out of bed when Rocky returned the next morning from PT and morning formation. He looked so amazing in his ACU's. I loved seeing him geared up in his uniform. He told me to get ready because we were meeting some of his buddies for lunch at Ruby Tuesdays. Rocky said one of his buddies was bringing his fiancé and they wanted us to meet each other. I got ready, and we left about thirty-five minutes later.

We pulled into the parking lot and parked the car. As we got out, Rocky said that he saw his buddy Tim Tarill getting out of his car with his fiancé. The sun was shining and he held my hand as we walked up. Tarill and his fiancé were walking toward the restaurant, too. We all stopped at the door and the guys lit up their cigarettes and Rocky introduced me to them. Two more walked up and met up with us as we walked inside. We only had to wait about five to ten minutes before we got seated.

After we were seated, Tarill's fiancé and I were talking. We got along instantly. Her name was Kendra and she was from Tennessee. She was so nice, and she had a little southern accent.

Our table got on the subject of her and Tarill's engagement because she brought up that no wedding plans had yet been made. They both stated that they would like to get married as soon as possible. It got quite noisy in the restaurant and we had to talk loud to converse.

As they kept talking about getting married, Rocky touched my shoulder and started to open his mouth like he was going to tell me something, but then didn't. I knew it was about us getting married. I thought he might want to be engaged again. After a while, still in the middle of the wedding topic, it happened again—he put his hand on my hand, seemed as if he was about to say something, and then didn't.

I just smiled at him. I didn't want to ask him what he was going to say because I wanted him to do this all on his own. I could feel it, though. It was most definitely about us getting married. All the wedding talk at the table got him thinking, I was one hundred percent sure. He wasn't going to bring it up tonight, though, I was pretty positive about that.

Kendra and I both ordered little slider burgers. I only ate a couple of bites because I started feeling nauseous. I did not think that I would start to get homesick, but it felt like I was. I started to feel overwhelmed and anxious. I just couldn't eat anymore, and even though I was having a great time and liked being out with these people, I kind of wanted to get out of there.

◆

A couple of days later, which was my fifth day there, Rocky and I were watching a movie. I was wrapped in a big blanket sitting on the floor against the bed, and he was sitting up on his bed, half watching the movie and half doing some work. His phone rang and he ran over to it and answered the call. I could hear him talking, and he was talking fast.

"We'll be right there," he said, hanging up the phone.

"What's going on?" I asked him.

"Tarill and Kendra are getting married right now! It's last minute, but we don't have time—we have to go! Get ready...just hurry, because we have to run out the door in five minutes!"

I was nowhere near ready, my hair was a mess, and I didn't know what to wear. I straightened my hair as fast as I could, but it was definitely not to my liking. I changed my clothes and we left in ten minutes instead of five.

When we arrived, they needed two witnesses. Witness number one was Rocky and witness number two was another one of Tarill's buddies.

It was a short and sweet ceremony, about twenty minutes long. After they were married, we went to a hotel to celebrate and have some drinks, and we all spent the night there. Rocky and I fell asleep on the floor. It felt like a dream that I was still there with Rocky. I didn't care that we slept on the floor of his friends' hotel room, I was just having so much fun being with him.

The next morning the guys had to leave real early to get ready for PT and morning formation. Rouda and Tarill came back as soon as morning formation was over, and when they walked in without Rocky I got a little nervous. Tarill said that Rocky went to the credit union to get a loan. I knew nothing about his plans to get a loan; I hoped he was really out getting a loan.

We had to leave the motel around 10:00 am because that was checkout time. Kendra, Rouda, Tarill and I went to get something to eat at Wendy's after we left the motel. I was feeling annoyed with Rocky because I barely know the three of them, so it was pretty awkward for me being stuck with them. As we were leaving Wendy's, Rocky showed up in the parking lot. I got into the truck and we headed back to the barracks.

He did not get a loan, and had his camel in the back of the truck that Gaeler supposedly had in her car. He told me that when he came back from the motor pool, it was in his truck. I didn't believe it for a second, but I just sat there pretending I did. This day was really disappointing so far.

The next morning when Rocky returned from morning formation and PT, he sat me down on his bed to talk to me.

"I need to tell you something. I have some bad news."

He looked sad and I started feeling nervous. He kept rubbing my upper back. I could tell something was up.

"Honey, I'm leaving," he said.

I just stared at him, very confused.

"I'm being deployed overseas. My unit is going to Iraq."

My first thought was that he was going to get hurt—or worse, killed. I asked him when they were leaving.

"It's looking like January 2nd" he said.

He was leaving before we could really get our relationship back to the way it was, and I didn't know how long he would be gone. He wrapped his arms around me and squeezed me tight. At that moment, the only thing

I knew was that he and I and had thirteen days left before he deployed. I didn't want our next thirteen days to end; I was starting to miss him already. How would things be 100% better in thirteen days?

We met up with Rouda, Tarill, and Kendra for brunch. I was happy I had met Kendra; we clicked right from the start. She was such a nice person, and we could relate well because we knew what each other was going through. After lunch, we stood in the parking lot a while so the guys could smoke their cigarettes.

They decided that we should meet over at this hotel called Value Place and get a room to stay in for the remainder of our time in South Carolina. We were going to share a room to save on money. The rooms came with two king-size beds and from what we had heard, they had a good amount of space. The hotel was off base but still relatively close to the base, only being about a 5 minute drive.

CHAPTER 17

We were down to having twelve days left. When they guys went to morning formation and PT, Kendra and I grabbed some coffee did a little grocery shopping for our room so we could cut down on eating out and save a little bit of money. Then we picked the guys up from morning formation. Since Kendra and Tarill were married, she had a Fort Jackson ID that let her go on and off post, without it we wouldn't have been able to do that.

When we got back to the hotel, Rocky told me to get ready because we had a meeting to go to regarding the deployment. The soldiers were to bring their spouses. I don't think it was mandatory because not everyone went, but Rocky wanted me to be at this meeting.

At the meeting, they talked about all sorts of stuff, from how we should spend the money while they were gone to joking around with us and even giving us tips. The sergeants told us that their unit would return in September, and repeatedly reminded us that they would be home no later than September. I was thankful to know when they would come home instead of having to go home wondering.

When the meeting was finished, Rocky introduced me to a few people on our way out of the building, and then we went back to the motel.

Tarill and Kendra were all ready to leave when we got back to the hotel. They said there was a party on base, so Rocky, Rouda and I got ready, too. We all piled into Kendra's car with the music blasting and

Tarill singing. When we got to the party, Kendra and I knew nobody so we followed each other around. It was a party with a bunch of soldiers and sergeants. We stayed for probably about an hour and a half.

For the rest of my time in South Carolina, nothing else happened with Morgan Gaeler except for finding out that they bought Rocky's chinchilla together; it was *theirs*. And he let me play with that thing? A total slap in the face! She demanded to have the chinchilla back or she was going to go to their First Sergeant, and when he went to return it to her he refused to let me come along. I had to stay with his buddy, Tymon in the parking lot.

Gaeler and Rocky were only at the other parking lot, so we could see them. I was really upset he made me stay behind; I wanted to see this girl face to face. Even Tymon thought he should have let me go with him. I just wanted her to see me. How could I know what they said to each other? He didn't have the best track record with me in the last few months!

Rocky told me they didn't speak a word, which I could maybe believe because I watched her grab it out of the truck and him pull away, but I couldn't make out whether they said anything or not.

This trip had flown by right before my eyes, and now we were on our way to meet with the other soldiers and sergeants as they were preparing to leave for Iraq. I wondered how we got to this point so fast. It seemed like just yesterday we were hanging out and I was dreading the day that he would leave for basic training. There I was getting ready to say goodbye to the love of my life, as he would soon be on his way to his first deployment, Iraq.

I had what seemed to be a billion things running through my brain. I wondered if I would ever see him again, if he would be okay, if he was going to get hurt. We pulled into the station, parked and got out. I was seventeen years old and not only was I there saying goodbye to Rocky, but also preparing myself to drive his truck from South Carolina all the way to Pennsylvania.

I was not good with directions. I couldn't find my way out of a paper bag. I was so thankful for Rocky's buddy Trumpler's mom, Sonja, for letting me follow behind her to Ohio because then I would only be one state away from home.

It was so early that it was still dark outside. We never went to bed that last night. I really should have gotten a little sleep before having to make the long drive home. I hoped that I would be okay. Rocky and I were just hanging out with all of his buddies, and taking a lot of pictures. I was honestly scared, scared to not be with Rocky and scared about my journey home. It was very chilly out, but I hardly noticed because my nerves were a mess.

Time just kept on flying by. I thought time was supposed to slow down when you were not having fun. Apparently that was not the case, because every time I checked the time it was closer and closer to them leaving. We would not be able to watch them board the plane; when it was time to say goodbye, they would get in a bus that would transport them to their plane.

Kendra and I kept glancing at each other with the same heartbroken look. At least we had each other and knew what each other was going through. I knew that I was going to really miss her. Honestly, this trip had probably been the best experience of my life, even with some negative events along the way, and I was so sad that it was ending.

Departure time was getting closer. Rocky called his parents to talk to them before he left. When he got off the phone, the sergeants yelled to the soldiers, letting them know it was time. Rocky grabbed me and squeezed me harder than he had ever hugged me, ever, and I squeezed him back. I was crying and he was telling me how much he loved me while I kept repeating how much I loved him.

They gave us about two minutes to say goodbye. We didn't let go until they called the soldiers. He gave me one last kiss and I stood there and watched him walk away to stand with the other soldiers. Kendra came to me and we stood there arm in arm and couldn't stop crying. The soldiers all boarded the buses and then they were gone.

Kendra and I turned around, and walked into the parking lot still arm in arm and still bawling like babies.

"Rose, we cannot lose touch with each other. We have to talk every day!"

"I know, Kendra. When you are feeling down, call me, and when I'm down I'll call you. I don't care if it's 3:00 in the morning, just call at any time."

We hugged goodbye, and just like that, Kendra was getting in her car and driving off. I ran over to Sonja. She hugged me and I hugged her, as she also had just said goodbye to her son. She said that she had to stop back at her hotel to grab her stuff before we left for home, so I headed on over to the truck and started it up. It was so weird to know I was all alone now with Rocky's truck; it was a horrible feeling. I let Sonja go ahead of me and I followed.

CHAPTER 18

When we got to Sonja's hotel, I ran upstairs with her and helped bring her things down. I was just anxious to begin the drive home. It was about 7 a.m. now and we were estimated to be home around 7 or 8 o' clock that night. It was about a 12 hour trip. Sonja pulled out of the parking lot and I followed behind.

As much as I hadn't wanted to leave South Carolina, everybody was gone now, so I just couldn't wait to get home. I was nervous. I had sixty dollars to my name, it was my first time driving a long distance basically by myself, and I had not slept in 24 hours.

I was driving behind Sonja and not feeling too tried. I was keeping up with her, but we were not on the throughway yet. Rocky left me his cell phone, which I was thankful for, so Sonja and I could keep in contact on the road if we needed to.

After two hours of driving past what looked to be fields all around us, we stopped our vehicles to figure out where we were. Sonja talked to a couple who were going into a gas station. I didn't hear much of what they said, but when Sonja walked over to the truck, she said we had been going the wrong way. I was thinking, *seriously? For two hours we have been going the wrong way, just our luck.*

I wasn't mad at Sonja, just at the situation. I was grateful to her because I still couldn't believe she was helping me get home, but getting lost would definitely add time to our trip. I guessed we wouldn't be getting home until ten or eleven now.

After I ran into the store and grabbed a coffee that I hoped would keep me alert, we turned around and headed back the other way. Once we got going in the right direction and got ourselves on the throughway, traffic moved fast and I was not used to it. My phone rang and it was Kendra calling me already, but I couldn't talk long because I had to concentrate on the road. It was so good to hear from her, though.

After a while, Sonja was hungry, so we stopped at a little pizza express. She bought me something to eat for lunch, too. I think she knew that I did not have much travel money. I was hoping we would eat while we kept driving so we wouldn't lose any more time, but she wanted to sit there and eat, so we sat outside and ate. About 25 minutes later, before we left, we took a picture together, then we started driving again.

Once we got into Virginia, we stopped at a gas station and I put 40 dollars into the truck. I didn't know how much tolls would be, so I didn't want to put the whole 60 dollars in. Back on the road, I began noticing that I was feeling more and more tired. I was also cold, but when I turned on the heat it made me even more tired, so I kept myself cold in hopes that it would help me stay more alert.

At one point, Sonja was flying and I couldn't keep up well enough. I missed the exit that she got off on. There were so many cars flying by. I pulled over onto the side of the road not knowing what to do, and I was so scared that I started freaking out. I thought I had lost Sonja for good, but thank goodness for cell phones because we got on the phone with each other and then not even ten minutes later, she found me pulled over. Needless to say, from then on I followed right behind her because I was definitely not taking a chance on losing her again.

The next gas station we stopped at was in West Virginia and I had to put the rest of my money in the tank. I had nothing left, forgetting about tolls. My papa kept calling me. He was already in Ohio waiting for me with my uncle and it was only 5:00 p.m. at that time. Unfortunately we got lost again, pushing our estimated time of arrival in Ohio to 1:00 a.m.

I was so tired, it was unbelievable. Sonja received an unexpected phone call that her husband was in the hospital. I felt very badly for her. She had just said goodbye to her son as he went on his first deployment, and then on the same day her husband was admitted into the hospital and she was about 8 hours away from being able to see him.

Sonja paid for my tolls and she even stopped and filled up my tank for me. I don't know what I would have done without her. I keep picturing my bed and how badly I just wanted to lie in it. I was also missing Rocky and wondered how he was doing. I had played the CD with Austin Winkler's music over and over again. The whole CD reminds me of Rocky because that is all we listened to. Every song on the cd is awesome. I never had to skip over any songs because I liked every song.

It felt like we would never make it home. I couldn't wait for this trip to end. Finally around 11:30 p.m., we were getting onto a Turnpike. By this time I was exhausted to the fullest extent. I could feel my eyes wanting to shut and I was really freaking out inside, but I couldn't stop it. I was starting to get delirious and delusional. I was saying the craziest things to myself and I did not know where it was all coming from. I started praying to God but mid-sentence I'd say something else that didn't make sense.

At this point, I needed to pull over and sleep; I didn't care if I lost Sonja. She had to get to her husband and I needed to shut my eyes—but there was nowhere to pull over on this turnpike and it just wouldn't end. I kept praying and praying, hoping that eventually there would be somewhere for me to pull over, but this turnpike only had two lanes and absolutely nowhere to pull over.

We were on the turnpike for nearly an hour until we finally reached the end of it, and about four or five minutes later we reached the hospital where Sonja's husband was, and where my uncle and papa were waiting for me.

It was so good to see them, but we still had about six hours of a driving to go before we would arrive home. My papa didn't want to keep Sonja long so she could get up to her husband, but he thanked her for everything and gave her $200.00. I got into his car, my uncle got into the truck, and we were on our way. It felt so good to be able to sleep.

CHAPTER 19

We arrived home at 6:00 a.m. Our twelve-hour trip had turned into a twenty-four-hour trip. Being home never felt so good. I went into the house and said hello to my grandmother, chatted for a minute or two and then went to my bedroom for more sleep.

I woke up the next morning and lay in my bed replaying the last two days over in my head for a good hour. I was so worried about Rocky and missed him so much. I wished it was two weeks ago when I was just getting to South Carolina.

I walked out into the kitchen to look into the driveway at Rocky's big, shiny, red truck. It was almost sad seeing it out there, but I was glad I had it because with me, I know it will be safe until he returns.

The days dragged, but the weeks were flying by. Kendra and I talked just about every day. I knew what she was going through and vice versa. In such a short time, she had become my good, good friend and I was so glad to have someone to go through this with.

Rocky got another cell phone. He was in Taji, Iraq. It was nice being able to talk to him a little more. He went out on missions; that was pretty much all that he could tell me on the phone. What he could say was very limited, and that was a little worrisome. While we were on the phone, I heard loud indescribable noises, men yelling and just pure chaos.

"I gotta go," Rocky yelled. "I love you."

And he hung up.

◆

I thought I was going to be sick. I was a wreck, expecting to hear the worst. Those next three hours were the longest three hours of my life. I just lay in my bed and cried until the phone rang and it was Rocky. They were attacked but I was thanking God to hear of no casualties on their part.

After we got off of the phone, I thought to myself, *how am I going to get through the next 8 months of him being gone?* I decided that I would make a calendar and plan something fun once a week so I always had something to look forward to. I hoped that might make time go by a little quicker. I also wanted to do a lot of wedding planning. I didn't want to buy the calendar, I just wanted to make it.

Every morning I would wake up and cross the day before off. Some days I would forget to do it, so when I would remember to do it later, crossing out more than one day at a time always felt so good.

Kendra and I had been talking about how eight months might seem like a long time away, but it really didn't give us that much time to have our apartments ready by the time the boys got back. I wanted to be moved out to South Carolina by the time Rocky came back from deployment. Kendra did, too, so we were going to plan our dates so that when I flew out, she drove up at the same time. She and I would get a hotel there or I would drive back with her to Tennessee and fly home from there, because she was only several hours away from Fort Jackson. Her dad was going to meet us in South Carolina and help us with apartment hunting, too.

Renza and Dom were doing well. I visited them a couple of times a week. Time was going slowly, yet so fast at the same time. One second I'm just moving to a new place with my family and meeting Rocky, the next second Rocky is in basic training and we're moving into an apartment and then shortly after that, moving again to a motel, and then when I blinked again Rocky goes overseas and I begin to live with my grandparents and can only see Dom and Renza once or twice a week—it was crazy!

CHAPTER 20

It had been six months since Rocky deployed. He didn't know when he'd come home on leave, but he was guessing September—that was what he was trying for. He was supposed to return in September, but now he was only looking forward to a leave because now they didn't plan to bring his troop home until April. I was still planning wedding details. We were going to get married while he was home on leave from Iraq.

The closer we got to the wedding, the more I started to think about the way he two-timed me before I went to South Carolina. I considered it two-timing because they were together so frequently. He could twist it and bend it anyway he'd like, but the truth of the matter was he put her feelings before mine. My heart had been broken when that went on and it was still a bit bruised.

I knew I would never know the truth about what the relationship between the two of them had actually been like, but I prayed to God that he was being honest about them just being great friends. I worried now because marriage is forever and if he could break my heart like that once, might he do it again? And to marry so soon after it all—but it was a chance I was going to take.

I wanted nothing more than to know that he never stepped out of our relationship and for us to be happy and soon married. Rocky knew that he didn't have to worry about me hurting him behind his back and I deserved not to have to worry either.

I worked a lot at the Ice cream shop, which was another way to make time go a bit quicker and not think about things so much. One night at work, Lisa, a girl that I work with, came up to me and told me that my ex-boyfriend had called the shop looking for me. She told him that I didn't work there anymore and didn't know any of my information; she told him that she thought that I might be in South Carolina visiting my boyfriend. I was happy she did that. She remembered what I went through with him and she never liked him because of certain things. She said that she loved being able to get rid of him for me.

Dino was my ex-boyfriend. When I met him he was charming and funny and very outgoing. The story of Dino goes a little something like this...

One evening I was sitting outside of my house with Bridget and another two of my closet girlfriends, Isabella and Lena. I was fifteen. Lena's boyfriend stopped over and then my cousin Nikki and our friend Katy happened to be walking by with a friend of theirs who was riding a bike.

The eight of us were just chit-chatting outside and then a friend of Lena's boyfriend was walking by, so he stopped too. This happened to be Dino, but I had never met him before. At the time, we lived on a busy street and people were always walking by my house. The guy on the bike asked me what my name was and how old I was. I smiled and responded "don't worry about it." I think I was just trying to show off for Dino.

Dino overheard my response to the guy's question, and he looked at me.

"What are you some kind of Beverly Hills chick?"

"Sure, and you can be my body guard," I said jokingly.

We both started laughing and exchanged names. All of us talked for a few more minutes, and in that few minutes I learned that Dino was 24. He did not look it whatsoever. He was my height, 5'3, maybe 5'4, tops and he had such a baby face. I swore he couldn't be more than 18!

Bridget, Isabella and I went into my house because dinner was done. They were spending the night. Everyone else left and Lena went to the store with her boyfriend. After my mom gave us our pizza and walked away, I could talk privately to the girls.

"Do you know who would be so cute if he wasn't 24?"

"That Dino kid!" they both blurted loudly.

About five minutes later, Lena came running in for her stuff.

"My mom's outside to pick me up, but Rose, that kid is outside, Dino. He's like waiting for you, and he said to come down."

The four of us got so excited.

"Oh my goodness, though, are you going to tell him how old you are?" Lena asked.

"I don't know!" I said excitedly.

We followed Lena out and she took off with her mom. Dino and I sat outside of my house talking from 9 p.m. to 4 a.m. Around 4 a.m., Dino said he was going to head home and told me that he lived right around the corner on Thompson Street, which was less than a five-minute walk. He asked for my number and I gave to him.

He started walking, and I was wishing he could stay longer.

"I kind of don't want him to leave!"

I told Izzy to chase after him and tell him to come back. Izzy and Bridget both went, but he had already turned the corner and they couldn't see him. It was really dark out.

I couldn't tell him my age when we were talking that night, I just couldn't. He told us that he had a five-year-old little girl and that he and his daughter's mother weren't together anymore. He said they tried making it work for their daughter, but just couldn't get along.

I liked him immediately but never had a chance to fall in love with him because over the next year it was just head games that he played with me and he toyed me around. It was about a month after he and I met when I finally told him how old I really was. He was mad at me and said it just wasn't for him. He went home but he called me the next day and said he had too many feelings for me to let me go.

I texted him one day after we had been seeing each other for about 6 months; this was when texting was a new cell phone feature. He couldn't text on his phone, but he could receive them. I got a phone call from his number shortly after I sent him the text message, but when I answered it, it was Rita, his daughter's mother, screaming at me.

According to her they WERE a couple. Later on that same day he called me saying that she was just jealous and crazy. I chose to believe him, but I shouldn't have.

As time went on, I kept catching on that he was being dishonest. Little things began to make me think... I hadn't met anyone in his family. There was a box of tampons in his bathroom. I was only allowed over on certain days and only at certain times. He never took me out and never bought me anything nice.

I knew that I should have let it be and let him work it out with her, but I was too far in and cared too much, so I chose to ignore the signs. Dino broke up with me once or twice a week for no reason, and then by the next day would call me back and make up with me. Every single time he broke up with me, I knew that he would call me the next day but it still hurt every time and he caused me so many tears.

He wouldn't meet any of my family, either. Everyone made fun of me and referred to him as my imaginary boyfriend. He kept telling me that it was because of my age that things had to be the way they were and that when I turned seventeen, we could go public. I was in denial, but deep down I knew he wasn't telling me the truth. I was just his side girl and he had no intention of having anything real with me, but I longed for my 17th birthday just in case he was telling the truth.

Dino and I finally ended when I found out that he was a newly married man. When I was at home waiting for his call because he was supposed to be away for the day and was going to call me at a particular time, he was actually at his wedding. It wasn't just a justice of the peace wedding. No, it was a big, fancy, Italian wedding.

He didn't have the nerve to tell me himself; I found out from a friend of his. Rocky, who was just my friend at that time, was sitting outside of my house with me while I was hurt over Dino. While Rocky and I were sitting on my front steps, Dino called me saying that he was forced into it and he had no choice or he wasn't going to be allowed to see his daughter. I was in tears and Rocky was rubbing my back.

"That's it, we can go public. You can even talk to Rita," Dino said, and he started to blurt out her cell phone number to me, but I didn't want it. In that moment, I realized that there I was crying over the biggest jerk when I had a pretty awesome guy sitting right next to me. This was someone who cared about my feelings, and sat there with me to make sure I was okay.

I told Dino to stay with Rita, and then I hung up. The next day I woke up thinking about Rocky but I wanted Rocky to come to me first, I didn't want him to think that he was a rebound. After a few weeks our texts changed from short messages about what time everyone was meeting up or what we were going to do, to conversations for hours and then after some time, to sweet ones. I got butterflies every time we were together, but I acted very nonchalant.

Then after another few weeks, he grabbed my hand for the first time and I'll never forget that feeling that I felt – the butterflies went crazy. I had waited so patiently for that to happen. A couple of days later we had our first kiss. We became inseparable, and I found out what real love felt like for the very first time. I had fallen harder for Rocky than I ever thought possible. It was the best feeling ever. I was so happy.

CHAPTER 21

I knew I would be moving to South Carolina soon. It was hard to accept that I would not be near my family, especially my grandparents. I loved them so much. Rocky had told me that he would put me on a plane home to see my family every few months because he knew how much they meant to me. That gave me a bit of comfort, knowing that I would not be only visiting them once a year, and I knew my grandparents would come and visit me, too.

I worried about Rocky constantly. I was not quite as scared as before, but sometimes I did think too much and scare myself. I was just so glad that he had a cell phone over there. Before he got a cell phone, he would use the telephones that were based off of other satellites I believe, so when he would call it would say he was calling from Texas or Florida. The first time I got really excited because I thought he was back stateside!

After work one afternoon, I walked over to the park to wait for Rocky to call me. I only had to work until 3 p.m. because I opened, and Rocky was supposed to call at 3:30 my time. The phone rang and I quickly answered. He said he only had about ten minutes to talk, so we talked a little about the wedding.

We both wanted the reception at The Comos, which was an amazing Italian Restaurant, and a favorite for both of our families. They had done weddings, showers, parties, you name it, for our families, and it was also a great place to just go out for dinner. I would not dream of having my reception at any other place. I grew up with my family doing everything at The Comos.

I loved Rocky's voice. He had the sweetest, most adorable, handsome voice. I missed him so much. About five minutes into the call, I could sense that he was itching to say something. Finally, Rocky spat out the words.

"Rose, I just can't go into a marriage with you while I've been hiding the truth about what really happened."

I instantly felt sick to my stomach.

"What happened?" I asked sadly.

"When we were hanging out..."

He hesitated, and I waited.

"When we were hanging out, we had sex."

The stress in his voice was nothing compared to what I was feeling. I sat the on the curb by the park and felt like throwing up. I had nothing to say.

"I'm sorry, Rose ...I'm so sorry..."

He just kept saying that he was sorry.

"I love you, Rose. I was afraid to tell you the truth before because I thought I would lose you, and I know I still might, but you deserved to know. I feel like the worst person in the world. I began pushing you away because I was ashamed. When I say I'm sorry I mean it. I'm so sorry I ever did this. I love you..."

"I loved you. I have to go, goodbye Rocky."

That was all I said back to him before i hung up. I was sad, then all of my thoughts turned my sadness into anger. I was furious because at sixteen years old I waited for him while he went to basic, to AIT, to ranger school, to Fort Jackson, and while he went to Iraq. He had a girl who would be nothing short of faithful while he was in all of those places.

All I did was work my butt off, and think of him, making hundreds of baked goods and sending them to him and his buddies overseas, planning our life together, making sure he knew he had a girl back home who was his rock.

When Dom and Renza did not have the money to fix the truck and to go down for his Basic graduation, one of the most important times in a soldier's life when a soldier needs to know he has someone out there in the crowd who is proud of him, you better believe I was working and saving every penny. I even saved enough to pay Brayden to watch Snickers while we were gone.

I became the most angry when I remembered how back in November, Rocky tried to turn our problems around on me. He had talked to me like I was a psycho for crying and arguing with him over Gaeler, and he had even said the wedding was off until I got my act together. He made me feel like I was the problem.

Rocky had put off our marriage for her, and that was the very worst part of it all. He had lied to me this whole time, and I was so angry. I had never felt that way before. My love for him changed as that memory took over. I never thought we would go through that. I should never have said I love you when we got off the phone, because now I hated him.

◆

I decided to show Rocky that he had made the biggest mistake of his life. I ran back to the ice cream shop while it rained on me. I went straight for the phone to look through the calls on the caller ID to find when my ex-boyfriend, Dino, called. I was going to call him. The only incoming call that I did not recognize was a long distance call from Louisiana. That was weird, but I called it anyway.

"Hello?"

I recognized Dino's voice.

"Hi, it's Rose. You called?"

"I've been trying to find you, but it's hard when I'm living all the way out in Louisiana now. I moved out here to be closer to my mom and brother. So, is it okay that I called you? I don't want to step on Rocky's toes."

"Well, normally no, that wouldn't be okay, but right now it doesn't matter so don't worry about it."

He said he was sorry, but I don't really think he was. I took the phone outside with me. Dino told me that his wife and his daughter had moved out there, too. According to him, he and Rita had been broken up for about five months and she had met someone else. He said that they were getting a divorce so she could marry her current boyfriend.

I knew Dino could be lying based on his history of lying to me in the past while really being in a relationship with her. Still, I had something to prove, so I gave him my cell phone number before hanging up. It felt wrong, and I didn't care.

Over the next couple of weeks, Dino and I talked and texted a lot. I usually didn't take Rocky's calls, and when I did, I was short with him. Just hearing Rocky's voice hurt me all over again. I could not stop thinking about what he had done to me, and I was angry and bitter. Even watching any show or movie with any romantic scenes made me cringe because I could just picture the two of them together. I wanted him to know what it felt like! He was starting to get a taste of his own medicine. He was feeling down because he noticed I did not talk to him that much anymore—just like when he did that to me.

I told Rocky that I needed a break from us. Now the tables were turned—I was ignoring him! It did not help that on the rare occasions when I did answer his calls, he had to bring her up and how he was sorry for what they did and what they put me through.

He even accidentally blurted out buying her flowers when I was down there just so she would act cool and not try to contact me or come by while I was there and tell me the truth. He said he told me the flowers part on purpose, but I think he accidentally said it and then had to finish.

Before long, Dino started talking about moving back and trying a relationship with me again. I did not want him to move back, I just wanted someone to help me get over Rocky. I told him to stay there with his daughter and that I'd come out there and visit him, though I had no actual intention of doing so.

Rocky kept calling me. I hated when I saw his name pop up on my cell phone screen. Dino kept calling me, too. I stopped taking Dino's calls. If Dino hadn't started talking about moving back, I would have kept talking to him. I knew I was wrong for trying to use Dino to get back at Rocky. I was sure that made me a hypocrite, but for once I didn't care. I was sick of being the one to get screwed over. I didn't know why I was trying to get back at Rocky anyway, because I was done with him!

I had been working ever since we opened; actually even before, to get everything ready.

Dino had not called me in two days and I had only talked to Rocky once. It was 4:00, time to punch out, go home and be miserable.

Rocky didn't know that I was talking to Dino, but even just being deceitful behind his back gave me a feeling of power, I had the upper hand with Rocky for once. The more that I made him feel like I didn't care about him the more he begged for me to love him again.

I walked outside of work after my shift and I couldn't believe my eyes. Was it really? It was! No! Dino was sitting outside in his car. I thought to myself, *Oh no, this just can't be!*

I walked over to Dino's car and he had a huge smile on his face.

"Are you surprised?"

I didn't even know what to say.

"Can we go get something to eat?" he asked.

"Sure," I said.

He took me to Long John Silver's. We got our food, sat down, and before we could start eating he grabbed my hands.

"Rose, I know I really screwed up in the past, but if I could take it all back I would. When you first saw me sitting outside of your work earlier, I got a reaction but not the reaction I thought I'd see. I chose the wrong girl back then and I am an idiot. I came all the way here for you. I want to show you that I can and will be the man you deserve, and you never have to worry again about me hurting you. I have never stopped loving you."

I just forced a smile.

"Aww," was all I could think of to say.

I really wanted to scream! What did I just get myself into? I didn't want this at all! Dino was the worst boyfriend in the history of boyfriends. Taking me out somewhere in public was new, though; he had never done that before.

After we ate, he dropped me off at home. I walked into my house feeling like I was carrying a huge weight my shoulders. I did not know how to fix this problem. I had led him on and I didn't know how to get out of this. How was this going to end up? As angry as I was at Rocky, I did not want to really be with Dino. I still loved Rocky, even though I felt like I hated him at the same time. The only good that had come out of talking to Dino was that it got my mind off of Rocky a bit.

At the moment, I was very confused. I thought I wanted to be done with Rocky, but then started to think that maybe I didn't. I couldn't understand why I was so confused. It's crazy how fast things can change. My feelings were hurt, and I was not in such a happy place anymore. For being such an angry girl with a broken heart, I should have been able to just tell Dino that I did not want to pursue anything with him, but yet, I just couldn't tell him. I wondered, *is anything right with me?*

A lightbulb suddenly came on in my head. Not that it was a good idea, but it was an idea. If Dino was anything like before, then I would not have to do much to get out of this mess. When Dino and I used to date a long time ago, he broke up with me all the time and for the most ridiculous reasons, too. All I had to do was wait for him to break up with me once, and I'd use that as my way to not see him anymore. Problem solved.

I could not believe that Dino had actually moved back out here to pursue a relationship with me. It was totally unlike him to do anything for me; maybe he had other motives for being back here.

CHAPTER 22

Dino had been here two weeks, and the guy had still not broken up with me. Even when I purposely got a little rude with him, he just kept treating me like gold and telling me how happy he was. This was not going to go my way, I could tell.

One night Rocky called after I began to feel guilty about what I was doing, so I answered his call. However, once we started talking I didn't feel guilty anymore because his voice was just a sore reminder of how he shattered my heart into a thousand pieces. He asked me if we could work on things, and I said no.

After we hung up, I started to feel bad again. He had sounded so sad. I started to think about him being overseas in Iraq. It was not going to be easy, but I also began to think that I should just suck it up and make him happy because he should be on top of his game there. I thought to myself, *what if something were to happen to him because he has his mind on me during missions?* As much as I felt that I hated him, I needed him to be okay. I decided that I would break if off when he got back from his deployment.

So I called him back, and when he answered, I said okay – let's work it out. I didn't warn him not to hurt me again or anything like that because this was only temporary; when he got back from overseas, I was done.

Rocky had pure excitement in his voice. If I hadn't known any better, I would have thought he sounded like he really did love me. It was almost sad to hear in his voice how happy he was. It made me feel bad again, but only for a minute. I just wished Dino had stayed put in Louisiana, but fine—he could get hurt, too, because he screwed me over pretty bad as well.

Really, I wasn't bothered anymore about Dino and everything he did to me, I was more than over it; however, I was so sick of being the sweet and over-caring girl who would get her heartbroken and stomped on. I said to myself, *I bet they don't even know what a broken heart feels like.* Maybe it was time they found out and maybe, just maybe, they would think twice about their actions the next time they want to be deceitful.

Dino was a great friend to his friends and the most happy, outgoing guy around; everybody loved Dino. You would never see him with anything other than a smile on his face, but for some reason, he had always enjoyed hurting my feelings! Maybe he had changed, I didn't know. It had been a while and I really didn't care, but I was not so sure people could change.

I didn't understand why Dino would leave his place and job to come here where he had barely any money, no place and no job. He started out sleeping at his grandmother's temporarily. After a week, he ended up running into an old buddy of his named Max who said that he could stay with him. Max didn't have much money, either. I helped take Dino's stuff to Max's place.

I felt bad when I noticed that there wasn't much food, so I went to the grocery store and bought them some groceries, and stopped at burger king and bought them some dinner for that night. When I took it to them, they were so grateful. I was starting to feel a little bit sorry for Dino.

My phone started to ring. It was Rocky. I hit ignore. Dino looked at me.

"Who was that, Rose?"

"Just my dad calling me back."

I left shortly after that. If I didn't answer when Rocky called me, I usually wouldn't be able to reach him when I called back because he called when he could and he normally didn't have long to talk. I called him back after and was surprised that he answered his phone. We talked for just

5 minutes. He asked me what I was doing. I lied and told him I was just leaving the ice cream shop.

I was doing the same thing to Rocky that he did to me, the same thing I was furious and hurt by, and now I was the one doing it. I couldn't help but start to think about the way that he did come clean on his own. I caught myself beginning to wish that I had just forgiven him. I should have, but I didn't, and now I had created a mess.

During that phone call, he told me that when he got back, I would see how sorry he was and that he already had ideas for us. He told me that I was the only thing that kept him going over there every day. I felt that he was being honest and genuine, and I knew in my heart that he meant every word.

When we hung up after that call, I realized that I completely regretted ever feeling like I wanted to get back at him. I really did want him back, and really in my heart, I was sorry. I had been blinded by the animosity, but I could finally see through it all. I knew that I had made a huge mistake.

One afternoon, Dino picked me up and said that he wanted to show me something, but wouldn't tell me where we were going. He pulled into this driveway and he said to me "you're going to finally meet my dad!" I couldn't believe it. This was something I had wanted at one point so badly, but now the timing was so wrong.

We got out and went in. I wondered what his dad thought of me, the once side chick, or did he ever know about me at all? Dino looked just like his dad, big Dino. His dad was warm and welcoming and just so nice. The three of us decided that we would have dinner together that night. Big Dino began cooking and I overheard Dino's dad tell him that Rita and his daughter were in town visiting and just got in that day. About an hour later I heard a little voice yelling "Papa! Papa! Daddy! Daddy!" She had such a sweet little voice. Here we go, though. I hoped that there wasn't going to be a brawl. I could hear Rita outside and she didn't sound happy.

Dino said, "Let's go outside with Hailey."

I knew it was sure to be awkward. We went onto the porch with her. Rita was outside standing next to her parked car with her boyfriend inside and her mother with her. They were talking to Big Dino. It was quite obvious that Rita had bad mouthed me at home, because when Dino said to Hailey, "Princess, I have someone that I want you to say hello to, this is

Daddy's girlfriend…" Hailey quickly cut in, "are you Rose?" I smiled and nodded my head. She walked up a little closer, stomped her foot, folder her arms and stuck her tongue out at me all at the same time, then turned around to walk away.

"Hailey! That wasn't nice at all! Rose is really nice and can do your hair all pretty for you and your nails…"

"Dino," I cut in, "it's okay. She's fine…don't push her."

Hailey was eight years old. She was beautiful, she looked like Dino's twin. Looking at Hailey was like looking at Dino.

Rita was furious that I was there and she kept lighting cigarette after cigarette. I felt like telling her *trust me, I don't want to be here either!* I couldn't quite hear what she was saying, but she was definitely venting about me. Dino was cracking up! I wasn't, though. It was an uncomfortable situation, and embarrassing. I was so happy when we left. It wasn't until then that I was able to laugh about it with Dino, but being there was too much.

Dino's insurance had lapsed the previous month when Rita didn't pay the insurance and got a new policy with just her car. He couldn't have his car on the road for a month because of the lapse. He had no car to drive and no money. He really would have been better off staying in Louisiana, but he just kept telling me that I was worth this hard time.

This was a completely different Dino than the one I used to know. Before Dino had to stop driving for a bit, he would cook me dinner and bring it to my job. I would get mad because I didn't want anyone to see him, but it was nice of him because the only thing Dino ever brought me to eat when we dated before—and one time only—was fries from a pizzeria. That was actually the only thing he ever bought me during our entire relationship.

CHAPTER 23

The 4th of July snuck up quickly and I was still in the same boat—lying to one, lying to the other, but keeping Rocky first. I was on my way to Dino's because we were going to go watch the fireworks. The more I started to feel sorry for Dino, the more I started to care about him. Were these pity feelings? Or was I catching some old feelings back?

As I walked up to the house, I noticed that Dino and Max were drinking, and Max was acting like he probably drank too much. They were hanging out outside. Dino was acting pretty rude to me. Maybe it was the alcohol. I didn't know what was going on with him, but the way that he was acting was getting pretty old quick. He had such an attitude toward me. He was completely ignoring me. It was starting to hurt my feelings a bit. Then Dino delivered the last straw.

"Rose, why don't you go home?"

I looked at him in shock.

"Fine!"

I started walking home, expecting him to yell for me to come back or run after me, but he didn't. He was just watching me walk away and he was smiling every time I looked back.

This was my out, but I didn't take it. Instead, I ran back to find out what his problem was. Why did I do that? It was the perfect opportunity for me to get out of whatever it was I was in with him. Was I really catching feelings? Why, why, why? I guess it made sense since we had been spending time together.

Well, Dino walked upstairs, and I followed him. Just as we were actually about to talk, Max started goofing around because he was completely drunk. He took his lighter and started spraying an aerosol can to get a big flame. Dino yelled at him to stop, and then we went into the bedroom to talk.

We did not even get to start talking in there, because the cops showed up for some reason. We could see them through the bedroom window. Dino told me to sit in the bedroom and he shut the door. He said he was going down to see what was going on.

From the sound of it, they were arresting Max—something about him throwing stuff onto the street. Who does that? Then I heard the sounds of glass breaking in the house. Was Dino breaking stuff? Was he mad at the cops for arresting Max? What an idiot. I didn't know what was going on, but I was not moving from that room. I wished that I had just left when he wanted me to go. *I* was the idiot.

All of a sudden, I heard screaming.

"Rose, Rose!"

I looked out the window and Dino was trying to run to into the apartment building. The cops grabbed him and threw him to the ground. I was embarrassed. I did not want to be associated with troublemakers. I had never known Dino and Max to act that way! I started to smell the sweetest smell, and I heard the cops asking frantically, "Is anyone else up in that house?"

Something clicked in my head, and I knew something was wrong and whatever it was, it was in the apartment. I slowly stood up and opened the door and walked out into the living room. A large sheet separated the living room from the dining room. I lifted it up and in front of me was a blazing kitchen and dining room.

I went into a kind of calm panic. I thought that I was done, though. The fire was huge—everything was engulfed in flames. After a few seconds of not being able to think, finally I turned around and ran back into the bedroom. I ripped out the screen and put my legs out the window, I wanted to jump but I was four stories up. The cops yelled for me to stay put.

"I'm jumping," I yelled back.

"Okay, jump on 3! 1, 2..."

I jumped on two. The two cops caught me, though I landed on my knee wrong. Dino ran to me and grabbed me. He wrapped his arms around me and would not let me go. The whole neighborhood was standing out there by the time I got out of the window. So many people came up to me; some were crying for me.

I watched Dino cry for the first time ever. He cried for me. I never smelled smoke and I never heard the explosion that they said happened in the kitchen. I only heard glass breaking and smelled sweet smells. What a 4th of July. What a night.

We had to go to the police station. When they were through talking to us, I called my mom and had her come get me. I wasn't sure where Dino was going to stay now, but Max's mom said he could stay at her house for a few nights. Max was hauled off to jail for a few nights.

I had the worst sleep ever that night. I could not sleep in the bed, I had to sleep next to a window. I was so paranoid over that fire, and I was afraid another fire would happen. I hoped that sleeping by a window wasn't going to be an every night thing for me.

Dino called me bright and early the next morning. He had some good news. He said this older man he used to help out all the time before he moved away, Johnny, offered him a bedroom at his house.

Dino had gotten good news, but two days later, I had gotten some not–so–good news when Rocky called me the next day. He had heard about the fire. He wanted to know why I was even there. He was really concerned that he did not know about me going anywhere for the 4th of July. He had seen Dino's name in the paper, too.

I told Rocky a lie. It seemed that I was doing a whole lot of lying. I told him that I went to a small 4th of July gathering with my girlfriends and that I didn't know that Dino would be there. I told him I didn't even say two words to Dino that night.

Rocky was pretty upset. I could hear it in his voice, but he didn't have much more to say. He wanted me to know that he felt a little uncomfortable with the whole thing, but at the end of the day he was just glad that I was okay over anything else.

CHAPTER 24

It was a beautiful, warm August morning. For the last few months, I had been with Dino all the time while still talking to Rocky. I was getting closer and closer with Dino, but I wanted to be with Rocky, too. I had to make the decision before Rocky came home. He didn't have any homecoming plans yet but I was sure they would be in the works anytime now.

I had kind of gotten over what happened with Rocky and Gaeler. When I was with Dino, all I thought about was Rocky. At home, all I thought about was Rocky. On the phone, all I thought about was Rocky. I'd had a perfect opportunity to break it off with Dino, and I wasn't smart about it whatsoever. Now I had to try to find another opportunity. This wasn't me! I didn't even know who I was anymore. I was so disgusted and disappointed in myself.

I cared about them both. I knew who I loved and wanted to marry, but I still cared for the other and felt sick about continually hurting him. For some reason that I couldn't understand, I loved how much older than me that Dino was. I liked our age difference. It was sort of hot to me, I didn't know why, but it was.

Actually the decision was an easy one to make; it was cutting the ties that was going to be difficult for me to do. It was easier when I was angry to hurt one of them, but as my anger decreased, it became harder to inflict emotional pain on them. I had blown my perfect opportunity to stop seeing Dino, but I knew that I couldn't blow the next opportunity. I hoped it wouldn't take too long for that next opportunity to present itself.

One night around midnight, we were sitting in the living room and Johnny was across the street at the bar. I wanted my life to go back to the way it was before I was so badly hurt. I wanted out of this mess that I had created. I did care about Dino, but at that moment I had finally gotten the courage to sit him down and tell him the truth.

"I have to tell you something, so just please listen."

I hesitated for a few seconds while Dino just stared at me.

"I am still talking to Rocky…"

Before I could say any more, Dino got upset, stood up and began yelling at me.

"Are you kidding me? I can't believe you, Rose! What the…are you serious?"

He got right in my face and screamed.

"ARE YOU SERIOUS?"

I got scared. He was freaking out, so I sugar coated it a bit.

"Well, I didn't want to upset him since he is in Iraq and needs to be in his right mind, not sad or hurting over me."

"Yeah, right…..you know what, I am done with you," Dino said as he walked into the bathroom.

I had an instant feeling that I needed to sneak out while he was in there. I crept slowly and as quietly as I could to the door, but he heard the door. He ran out of the bathroom as I ran out the door. I was running down the street, but he was right behind me. He caught up with me and grabbed me by the arm.

"Rose, get in the house. Get in the house now!"

He was talking in that voice where you "yell" but in a quiet manner, teeth showing and using a very angry voice.

"It's after midnight. And one more thing, don't you *ever* think about running away from me."

He was scaring me. He looked like pain and anger were at war inside of him, and anger was winning. I thought about it. It was sprinkling outside. I really had nowhere to go. It was too late to go to my grandparents. I just stared at him and nodded my head. He wasn't going to let me go anyway. Dino looked so mean. I had not seen this side of him before.

All of a sudden, he raised his hand and slapped me in the face. I was in disbelief, in shock. I couldn't believe that I had really just been slapped in the face by a man. I couldn't help but begin to cry, while standing in the rain with his hand grabbing my arm so tight.

"How could you do that?" I asked through my tears.

It started to rain even harder and Dino yanked me toward the house. Johnny was walking back as we were walking in.

After a little while of quietly sitting in the living room, Dino started talking to me.

"Rose, I'm sorry. I'm so sorry! I'll never hit you again…"

He kept telling me that over and over, but I just couldn't wait until morning when I could leave. When he drove me home the next morning, it was a quiet ride. I couldn't stop thinking about the night before, and the more I thought about it, the more I realized that he had started drinking quite a bit more than usual. I rarely ever saw him without a drink in his hand. As we pulled into the driveway, he was telling me that he would make it up to me and asked how he could make it better. I decided that I would tell him over the phone what I had already decided. I stepped out of the car and walked into the house. I had tried hiding what was going on with me and Dino, but my grandparents were catching on and they were starting to get a bit fed up with me. Heck, *I* was fed up with me.

While getting ready for work, I heard the doorbell so I ran to get it. It was Dino standing there with a single rose, a card, and chocolate. He gave it all to me and kissed me on the cheek.

"You mean everything to me. I love you and I hope I will see you after work."

I did not say one word. I shut the door, walked back to my room, fell on my bed and started to cry. I was in so deep. I had been betrayed by my fiancé, so I tried to give him a taste of his own medicine with my ex, Dino, who had also betrayed me before. Now it was all blowing up in my face. Dino had unexpectedly come back to home to Pennsylvania, I caught some old feelings, and now I wasn't able to break up with the one that I really want to break up with. I just didn't know what to do.

◆

After another couple of weeks went by, I was still seeing Dino, but still my heart was with Rocky. The feelings I had for Dino did not compare to my feelings for Rocky, but they were enough to keep me from breaking it off with Dino because I wasn't strong or brave enough to do what I needed to do, I didn't have it in me to hurt him.

It's easier to hurt two people behind their backs than to hurt one person to their knowledge. Even though Dino had hit my face, I cared for him and breaking up with him was much easier said than done.

I had to figure this out soon. August 10th had arrived. I was giving myself until September 1st to break it off with Dino. I figured that would give me plenty of time to come up with something. I felt a little sense of relief just having a date picked out, knowing that it would all be over soon.

When Rocky would call me, I would just ache with missing him. I wished so badly that I had never called Dino that night at the ice cream shop. What had I been thinking?! We all make mistakes; I should have just forgiven Rocky for his.

Over the next couple of weeks, Dino had taken me all sorts of places. He took me to a popular beach nearby—restaurants, but not just any restaurants. They were the best and fanciest places he could look up within a two-hour radius, and we'd make a little road trip of it.

He took me to this popular beach about two hours away. It's a pretty awesome beach with bars and restaurants. I had just turned 18 the month before in July, so I still wasn't legal to go to the bars but the perks of Dino being 27 years old was that he could go in and bring me out a cute beachy cocktail.

My favorite destination that we visited was when he took me to the Peninsula, a couple of hours away in Pennsylvania at the Presque Isle State Park. It had eleven miles of beaches. I loved it, and we really did have so much fun.

CHAPTER

It was 1 o'clock in the afternoon on August 25th. Dino had just picked me up to go over to Johnny's. Johnny was going to be gone all day—doing what, I didn't know. We stopped at the gas station, and Dino came out with three 40-ounce beers.

"What do you want to have all that for," I asked him.

"Because I can," he replied.

"I'm just concerned about you, that's all."

"Oh, yeah? Concerned about what?" he asked while laughing at me.

"You're drinking so much all of the time now, like, you always have a beer."

"I like my beer, always have."

"Well, how come I have never seen you drink so much like this before?"

"Well, Rose," he said in the snottiest, most mocking way, "I hardly spent any time with you before, so you don't know much of what I did."

◆

At seven o'clock, Dino had already walked to Wilson Farms for more beer. He came walking in from the store and his mood was no better.

"Hey, look what I got! There isn't a problem is there?" Purposely being rude.

"Nope, but I think *you* got a problem!" I said while glancing at the beer.

"Shut up, Rose."

I was getting so fed up with his rudeness.

"I'm leaving. I'll walk home before it gets dark."

"You are not going anywhere!"

Dino came over to me and pushed me downward to make me sit on the couch.

"Dino, I don't want to fight with you. I will go home and we can both cool down."

"Fine, go home… leave!"

I grabbed my purse and headed for the door. He followed behind me.

"You're really going to leave?"

He grabbed my arm and whipped me back towards him.

"Knock it off!" I demanded.

Before I could say another thing, he hit me as hard as he could in the nose. It hurt so much, I was bleeding and tears started flying down my face faster than a downpour of rain. I wasn't sure what that was, a punch or a slap, but it felt like my nose was broken. I was crying and kept telling him to get away from me. "Baby, I'm so sorry! Are you ok? I hate myself, please forgive me. I just don't want you to leave me. I need you, my Rose. I feel like you're going to leave me, and I can't take it. Maybe that's why I've been drinking a little more lately, I admit it, but I can't let you leave me. I just can't."

I just sat there without answering him, still crying. He went into the bathroom and poured his beers out; I could see he really felt sorry, but for him to be driven to the point of placing his hurtful hands to my face was completely unacceptable. I knew that I wasn't deserving of that… or maybe I was. When I looked into the mirror, I noticed my eyes were turning black and blue, he had hit me that hard. Hopefully they weren't going to look like that by morning because I really didn't want anybody to see me that way.

The next morning, Dino had already left by the time that I woke up. As I was trying to wake up, I started looking through pictures in my camera. I turned it back to camera mode and took some pictures of my face.

Dino came walking in with some cover-up makeup for me.

"I can't believe your eyes turned black and blue like that...I didn't even hit you that hard," he said.

But he definitely did hit me that hard. He grabbed my camera from me and deleted the pictures I had taken of my black eyes. Now he was angry that I took pictures of my face. He probably thought I was going to show everyone.

After about thirty minutes, Dino was being especially sweet to me. I didn't know what was going on with him. He was hot one minute and cold the next. I was thinking that maybe I never really knew Dino at all. I couldn't recall him having a violent bone in his body toward me or anyone else before!

I tried to understand. I knew he had to be frustrated knowing I was still talking to Rocky, but I figured that I had given him an excuse he should have been able to accept. Sometimes he treated me like he really loved me, but then other times one wrong word would set him off to the point that I really felt in danger. The longer that I stayed, the hole that I was digging myself into was becoming deeper and deeper.

CHAPTER 26

I went home the day after Dino gave me two black eyes. My makeup was carefully applied to hide the bruising. I hadn't been spending much time at home and I slept out often because my grandparents were so angry with me and my papa was always yelling at me for the way I was acting. I was changing and they were becoming more disappointed in me with every day that passed. Things just weren't okay.

I started cleaning my room and re-organizing my closet, figuring it would get my mind off of things. I felt so mad at myself because I had the chance to end things with Dino and I didn't, and I was beginning to become scared of him—scared of making him angry at me.

A bag full of Rocky's stuff from South Carolina was in my closet—I had taken it out of the truck before I gave his truck to Renza and Dom to drive because they sold the Camaro a few months before and my papa bought me a white ford Taurus. I started thinking about old times with Rocky and wishing things could just go back to the way they used to be.

I opened up the duffle bag and smiled as I pulled out some pictures. It was my first time opening it up. Looking at the pictures made me miss him even more. It looked like the rest of the bag was just his clothes. I figured I would wash them and hang them up in my closet; it would make me feel a bit closer to him.

As I was pulling out his shirts and pants, I pulled out two pairs of black shorts. I decided to check the size on the tag since I could plainly see that these were way too small for Rocky to be wearing. Size small on the tag. I knew that they couldn't be Rocky's. I knew that I had been being deceitful myself, but it still stung hard to know that I had her shorts with me for the entire time that I had been home from South Carolina.

I felt devastated. I walked to the gas station and bought a six-pack of beer. I was underage, but I knew all of the workers there and they didn't care because they could see that I needed one and they all thought I was the sweetest thing…if they only knew.

I started drinking, and after three beers I called Dino to come pick me up. I didn't know why I drank when I was sad, because it only saddened me more and made me think too much about all of my problems—not to mention that I didn't think clearly when I drank, but then again, nobody does.

When Dino picked me up, we drove to Johnny's. Dino and I hardly spoke. When we got there, I walked right into the living room and sat with Johnny. Dino didn't follow me in, but he texted me from outside and said he was going to the store for more beer.

I cried to Johnny and told him everything—everything about Rocky, everything about the banks and everything about Dino. I didn't even realize what I was saying until I was saying it. I couldn't shut up.

Johnny was the first person that I had talked to about everything, the first ear that listened, and the first shoulder I cried on. I felt a sense of relief and I knew my secrets were safe with Johnny, but I still regretted that I told him about the banks. I really should have left that out, but I was just pouring my heart out and it felt good.

Johnny told me that he loved Dino like a brother. He asked me if Rocky ever laid his hands on me like Dino did and I told him that he never did nor would, and then he told me that Rocky is who he wants to see me with.

Johnny told me that if he had ever seen Dino hurt me, he would have let him have it. He also said that he was disappointed in me for playing with both of their feelings. He told me that I had no business doing that, and that I had to come clean soon, but he wasn't telling me anything I didn't already know.

I felt like I was in too deep, and I didn't know where or how to start cleaning up the mess I had made. I couldn't wait for the day when this mess was no longer a problem in my life.

The next thing I knew, Dino came walking into the living room. We never even heard him come in through the door. He said something about forgetting to go to the bank; I didn't even realize that he had a bank account. He looked like he was up to something. He had an evil grin on his face. I spoke first.

"Dino, can we just have a good night, and we'll talk tomorrow?"

"Nah," he said, drinking his beer. "Well, wait, where did you want to talk? We could go talk at the bank..."

"What are you talking about?"

I wondered if he had heard anything Johnny and I had said. I told myself that he couldn't have, but I felt like he did hear.

"Oh, nothing," he said.

A minute or so passed.

"I feel like going for a walk...anyone care to join? We can take a walk to the bank."

Johnny answered, "Dino, cut it out. What are you getting at? Come on, be upfront."

Dino shot a look at Johnny.

"What do you know about being upfront? I heard you tell her to leave me, Johnny! You told the girl I love to leave me!

"Well, you're always beating her! You should find someone who doesn't make you want to beat her!"

And then Johnny turned to me.

"Not saying you do anything wrong at all to deserve it, because you don't deserve it..."

Dino cut Johnny off.

"Don't even sit there and comment on something that you know nothing about!"

Then he looked at me and I just knew that he knew, everything.

"By the way, if you're wondering, yes—I heard every last word you guys said. I know about everything, and I mean everything."

I started shaking and begging him not to say anything. I knew it, I knew he had heard. I sat there in denial until Dino had confirmed my fear. Johnny and Dino began to argue. I sat there feeling nervous. I felt like I was going to be sick. *What did I just do?* I just kept digging myself deeper and deeper.

"Rocky better stay away from you—that's the only way I won't tell!"

But I had a sick feeling in my gut. I wished so badly that I could take the whole night back.

Later on that night, Dino told me that he did not like the way I had gotten so upset over Rocky, and hated the way that I tried to protect him. Dino never went to the store that night. He said that he changed his mind and came into the apartment to see if I wanted to go out to dinner and a movie, but then overheard us talking.

I tried to be extra sweet so hopefully Dino would just forget about everything. I doubted that would happen, but I was hopeful anyway. When Dino and I went bed, he kept throwing little stabs at me about it all. I asked him to just drop it numerous times, but after a long time of arguing he decided to grab me by the neck and started choking me.

He let go of my neck finally, but then he grabbed my arms and held me down. I was crying, yelling and trying to fight him off. I was panicking and hoping that Johnny would hear us, but I knew that he was probably sleeping and he sleeps through anything.

I thought that Dino was going to kill me! He grabbed my head and pushed it backwards against the wall, and then positioned me on the bed so that my head and neck were off of the bed and he was pushing my head and neck down backwards. I was so scared! It felt like he was going to snap my neck!

After what felt like an hour, but was probably only several minutes, he finally calmed down enough to let me go. My neck was in so much pain.

I was too upset to go to sleep. *I should get out of here, run away from him and never look back.* But even though I knew there was no excuse for the violent way he had been treating me, I also knew I had driven him to it by using him to pay Rocky back. Now Dino really loved me and I just couldn't feel the same for him.

Dino wasn't that great at discussing things, so I guessed frustration made him talk using his hands on me instead. But he seemed to get so out of control, sometimes, I thought he really might go too far. What would next time be like, I wondered while I lay in bed next to him. I had no business going there that night. It only messed things up even more.

I couldn't leave in the middle of the night. I realized that I was scared of him. I thought he had the potential to be very dangerous—I could see it in his eyes and on his face. He would get this really vicious look, like a human pit bull. His facial structure really did resemble one; he was proud of it, too.

Before I went to sleep, I decided that I really needed to get out. I was in a rut that I did not know how to get out of. I was worried about Dino going to the authorities regarding the banks. Even though he claimed to not be the kind of person who rats on people, this situation was different. He made it quite obvious that he wouldn't hesitate much if it came to turning Rocky in. I just didn't trust him. He was becoming too obsessed with me, and it was scary.

CHAPTER 27

I called Rocky and told him about the discovery that I made in his duffel bag. They were Rocky's shorts, they were not hers. I believed him, he was telling the truth. They didn't wear long shorts when they ran for PT, they did wear smaller ones. If I would have called him right away instead of jumping to conclusions, that last night would have never have happened the way that it did.

Dino had gotten really upset with Johnny was after he eavesdropped on us that one night. He was so upset that he started looking for another apartment. He felt that Johnny wasn't being a good friend to him, but I don't think Dino realized at the time that Johnny was one of the best friends that he'd ever have. Johnny was just a very blunt person and Dino was too sensitive.

Dino found a little apartment down the street, about a four or five minute walk from Johnny's. I helped him move all of his stuff over to the new place—it really wasn't much. We loaded it all into the car in one trip.

Back at Dino's new apartment, I was helping to unpack his things. He was on beer number four, and not the 8 oz. size—he was drinking the 40 oz. glass bottles. As sweetly as I possibly could, I asked him to please stop drinking for the night. The reason I asked him was because he rarely didn't have a drink in his hand and I was hoping if he stopped drinking, maybe he wouldn't be so violent with me. Plus, I wanted to talk about us going our own separate ways, and taking a break. I wanted to tell him that it was just so I could focus on getting my life together. I didn't want him to think it had to do with Rocky; I didn't want him getting mad and turning Rocky in.

He just chuckled at me, and didn't say a word. He kept getting drunker and meaner, so I knew that I wouldn't be able to have a successful talk with him.

About an hour later, I told him that I was hungry. I wanted to go somewhere and grab a bite to eat. He pulled out one single packet of Ramen noodles.

"Dino, we don't even have a pan to cook this with, okay? So I want to go get something…"

"We have a bowl and a microwave, and that's good enough for you."

He filled up the bowl with water, emptied the contents of the Ramen noodle package into the bowl, and put the whole thing in the microwave.

"I am not eating that," I told him, and went back to unpacking.

After a few minutes, he told me to come and eat because my soup was done. I told him that I wasn't hungry. Dino came from behind and grabbed my arm and forcefully pulled me to sit in a chair and he set my bowl of soup on a little plastic table in front of me.

"Dino, stop! Why are you trying to make me eat this? I'm not hungry anymore!"

I watched him drop his cigarette ash into the bowl of soup and stir it around with the fork. He took a step back to stand behind me. Then he squeezed the back of my neck hard.

"Eat it now!"

He was really hurting my neck. I couldn't believe what was going on, but I leaned over and took a tiny bite.

"Dino, please! I am not hungry and I don't want to eat something that you dropped your ashes in! Who does that?"

He squeezed my neck again but less painfully this time; I thought it was more of a warning. He dropped ashes into the soup again and again, stirring each time with my fork. He finished his cigarette and lit up another one. He made me eat every single bite!

I couldn't believe that I didn't throw up, but I gagged so many times and my stomach hurt so badly. When I finished, he pushed me out of the chair. I just felt worthless and sick. How did a girl like me manage to get herself into a situation like this? I felt so sad.

Dino decided he wanted to go get something to eat for himself. I wished I could make *him* eat soup mixed with cigarette ashes. He made me go with him so I wouldn't try to escape. I felt like a prisoner, but I just kept telling myself that if I left, I would risk Rocky and Renza getting turned in for the bank thefts. It was just better that I stayed until I could somehow get him to agree to go our separate ways. Now that I actually had no problem with the idea of getting out of there and away from him for good, I had another reason holding me back.

While we were out, Dino's cousin called him and said he was stuck on the Boulevard because his vehicle broke down, so we had to drive 20 minutes to pick him up, then drive him home. On our way home, Dino let me drive. This was a relief, because he had drunk too much and couldn't even speak correctly.

We were on the throughway about ten minutes from home and he turned up the music. I turned it back down.

"I can't hear music right now."

Unfortunately, that's when my cell phone started to go off in my purse. Usually I kept my phone hidden and on silent. I'd usually say that I didn't carry it with me, but somehow it wasn't on silent anymore. Inside I was panicking and totally freaking out because it was probably Rocky.

My purse was right in front of Dino's feet on the passenger side and he started searching for my ringing phone. I was nervous. I couldn't figure out why it went off, but it was just my luck. Of course it was Rocky calling, and Dino answered. I couldn't hear what Rocky was saying but I knew I was so screwed.

Dino started to tell Rocky everything and instead of listening to them argue like I thought would happen, the two of them seemed to be getting along. And there I was, wondering what was going on.

After a minute or two, Dino said to Rocky, "We have to stick together, you and me, because this girl is playing games with the both of us. We have to help each other and both stay away from her." I know that Rocky asked to talk to me because then I heard Dino say, "No, you don't want to talk to her. When we get out of this car, I'm done with her too."

Contrary to what they said, neither one was done with me. I had them both wrapped around my finger. When they hung up Dino slapped me in the face. I started to cry because I was driving and he had just hit me on the thruway. I started to apologize because I was scared and wanted him to stop but he hit me again. I kept crying and yelling for him to stop. After the third time that he hit me, I was in hysterics.

When we pulled up to the apartment it was late; it was dark out. We both got out, and I wanted to run away at this point. I didn't want him to say anything about the banks and I was afraid that he would come after me, but I just couldn't be there with him anymore. I was frightened of what would happen after walking into that apartment.

As he was walking up the front porch stairs, I made a run for it. He ran after me and caught me immediately. He dragged me back by my arm and my shirt. Dino was little, but so strong. I was being dragged up the front porch stairs yelling, and no one heard me. I fought it so hard but he wouldn't let me go. The closer we got to that door, the more scared I became. I was panicking because I was so afraid of what was going to happen to me inside. I was not going into that apartment with him.

I pushed him off of me with all of my might, and he tripped on the top stair. I ran as fast as I possibly could. He was right behind me, but I didn't look back. I ran across the street and that was where he caught me. We both fell to the ground and as we fell, a man's voice yelled.

"What's going on?"

I heard him tell his wife to get into their car (they were parked on the side of the street) and grab the phone to call the cops. Dino started crying.

"Rose, please, I can't go to jail! Please don't let me go to jail!"

If he went to jail, then he might say something about Rocky and him mom. This was my perfect chance to get away from him and feel safe again, though. It would not be hard not to stay with that couple and wait for the police.

"Let's go," I told him.

We both ran back across the street, got in his car and drove off. The couple who called the cops got into their car and chased us, but we lost them. Whoever they were, I was grateful, because after that, Dino let me go home to my grandparents. It felt so good to be home.

CHAPTER 28

I was slowly talking to Dino less and less, but it wasn't easy because he was starting to become irritated with how little I talked to him and saw him. One night Dino kept calling me and I kept hitting ignore, because I was trying to reach Rocky. I didn't want him to be mad at me, I wanted him to forgive me. I didn't want to do this anymore, I loved him, I needed him and I couldn't deny it. Talking to him was all that I could think about.

Dino kept calling and was driving me nuts so I finally answered and he demanded to know what I was doing and why I wasn't answering the phone. I told him that I was in the shower. I had a gut feeling that I'd better wet my hair, so while we were on the phone, I walked into the bathroom, muted the phone while he kept talking, and stuck my head under the running bath water, then wrapped a towel around my hair.

The second that I un-muted the phone, my gut feeling materialized.

"Come to your window" Dino said.

I went into my room and opened up my window.

"Let me feel your hair."

I took the towel off and let him feel it. The look on his face was priceless, because he didn't believe me at first. He expected my hair to be dry. Then he wanted to come into my room, but I wouldn't let him.

Dino grabbed me. I didn't know if he was trying to pull me out of the window or pull his way in, but he wouldn't let go. I punched him in the face and he still wouldn't let me go so I took his hat off and threw it. He loved his hats and liked nothing dirty. I knew once I threw it he would probably let me go. I hurried up and shut the window and locked it, and he very angrily walked away.

I knew how to get into Dino's voicemail so later that night I made my number private so he wouldn't answer the phone and I could access it. I had a feeling that he and Rocky were communicating because Rocky wasn't taking my calls. There was one new voicemail and I listened to it, it was Rocky. "Hey it's me returning your call, give me a call later. By the way, when I come home on leave, the first round is on me buddy."

I laughed, I had to. I couldn't believe that I had turned them into friends. I was sure it couldn't last, although they really sounded like they would get along and they clicked when I heard them on the phone together, like they sympathized with each other. They could be as compatible as two matching puzzle pieces, but throw a girl into the mix and it wouldn't matter anymore.

Rocky finally took my call later that night and he was so angry with me. I came spic and span clean and told him everything that there was to tell, leaving nothing out. To my surprise, he said that he was going to forgive me. He also said that it was his fault that I did everything that I did, but I felt that the fault was truly mine. How could I have put such an amazing guy through all of that? He hurt me, yes, but he was still a wonderful person. He just made some bad choices.

I was out of control with everything I had done. He was a bit hurt, though, even though he had forgiven me because I left nothing out. I was so sorry, for everything. I was done playing games. I didn't want to be that person anymore – I was just right the way I was before, sweet and caring. I wanted to be that girl again.

The next afternoon, my grandmother said that she needed to talk to me. Now mind you, my grandmother works for VIP (Value in Pharmaceuticals), so she is educated on just about every prescription drug out there.

"Rose, did you take Dino to pick up any of his prescriptions lately?"

"No, why?" I responded a bit confused.

"I found Dino's bag that his medicine came in just lying in the driveway. Did you know that he has schizophrenia?"

"What? Are you sure?"

"Yes he does, and he must've dropped the bag out of his car."

After that conversation, things started making more sense to me. He would get angry and sad and angry and sad, and only would be happy some of the time. He would put things into his head and convince himself of things that made absolutely no sense, and you could only sit there and wonder how his mind come to such a conclusion. He was getting angrier and angrier and couldn't handle sadness.

Dino had a mental illness and he felt that he didn't need to take his medicine. Finally, it all made sense. That's why I heard him one day saying that when he goes to his appointments, he takes out the correct amount of pills and tosses them away to make it look like he had been taking the amount he should have taken. Without his medicine, he had the potential to be very dangerous toward others and to himself.

I knew I needed to be gentle with him; he wouldn't be able to handle a hard break up. I knew this was a delicate situation. I understood now why he was physically abusing me. I was breaking his heart and his schizophrenic mind couldn't handle it without the medication that he figured he didn't need.

◆

A few days later at around noon, I was all ready for the day with nothing to do. Rocky called me and said that Dino called him and he told Dino that he forgave me. He said that Dino sounded very unhappy as they got off of the phone. He said that it was a conversation with very few words.

Dino called an hour or so later and wanted to go get some coffee, so I said okay. It was time that I had another conversation with him. I didn't want to keep going on the way things were. I didn't want to keep hurting Dino. He didn't deserve another minute of it.

It was time that everything started going back in the right direction. Physically hurting someone is wrong, but in Dino's case, he couldn't control the way that he acted. He wasn't being smart about not taking his medication but his mind wasn't right and it wasn't his fault. Without that medicine in his body, he had absolutely no control.

Dino probably was taking his medication a few years before and that's why his personality was so drastically different now. It didn't help that he had someone playing games with his already unstable mind, but I didn't want to play these games anymore.

When he picked me up, he was crying. I didn't know how I was going to talk to him when he was upset. I kept asking him what was wrong, but he just kept reiterating the same thing.

"Nothing, I just love you."

After coffee, we went for a short drive. I thought we were just driving to no place in particular while I let him talk. It seemed like he was starting to feel better. I was waiting for him to get in the mood where I could attempt a serious conversation, but we pulled up to a police station instead. Immediately I looked at him.

"No, Dino, no, please!"

But he got out of the car anyway and then actually walked through the doors. I didn't know what to do. *Should I get out and leave or sit here?* My heart was in my stomach. I was so nervous, feeling like I could just throw up at any second.

Ten minutes later, Dino came out and said Officer Ray wanted to see me inside. I did not have to say much to Dino; he could read the words *"I hate you"* in my eyes, I was sure.

"How could you?" I asked.

He didn't respond. I didn't know what I would be facing inside. Rocky was going to hate me. He was going to get kicked out of the army and his career would be ruined, and it was all my fault.

When I got inside, they made me sit and they asked me questions. I couldn't lie, although I really wanted to, but I kept my answers as short as I could. Officer Ray walked out of the room for a couple of minutes and when he came back, he gave me quite the serious look.

"Listen, Rose, there was an anonymous tip describing you to a T, saying *you* were responsible for those bank robberies.

"No, that's not right, that can't be true!"

"Oh, it's true!" Officer Ray said.

I wondered, *was Renza trying to pin the banks on me? Was she afraid that she would eventually get caught? Maybe the cops were making it up or maybe* Dino *called in a tip!* All of these different thoughts were running through my brain.

The next day, the FBI called me and said that I needed to meet them somewhere, so we met at Burger King. I had to sit in their vehicle. I answered all of their questions. I told them how the Army was everything to Rocky and all of this happened before the Army. I told them Rocky was just trying to save his dad's life, his mom hadn't wanted to ask him to do it, but desperate times call for desperate measures. What they did was wrong, completely wrong, there was nothing right about it; however, it wasn't because they thought they are entitled to money they didn't earn. It was an awful idea that seemed like the only way out for Renza, and she regretted bringing her son and his friend into it every day.

"Please don't let this ruin Rocky's career, they are so remorseful!" I begged. "He is a good man! I promise you guys, he would do anything to help anybody!"

"Ma'am, we promise you he will not get kicked out of the army for this," the FBI agent sitting in the driver's seat said. I thanked them. I was so relieved to hear that.

CHAPTER 29

The federal agents had asked me not to say anything to Rocky, but as soon as I got home I called him. I was going to warn him—I had to. I called and he picked up.

"Rocky, you are going to hate me, but it got out about the banks and they are going to come talk to you."

Rocky did not even sound mad at me, to my surprise.

"I'll see you in a couple of days," he said.

"No, they promised that nothing would happen to your Army career... you are not getting kicked out of the army!"

"Rose, I'm telling you I'll see you in a couple of days."

He told me that he loved me, and I told him to act shocked because he wasn't supposed to know anything. I thought he would hate me but even after what I let happen, he was still so sweet with me on the phone. I was so sorry for this awful situation. I knew I had been the worst girlfriend in the whole world this last little bit, but I loved that boy more than anything.

Three days after I warned Rocky that the bank robberies had gotten out to the police, he had his gun taken from him overseas, meaning he was in harm's way with no way to protect himself for two and a half weeks. Then he was arrested over there and brought back to South Carolina where he had to stay on base until he was cleared out of the Army. They were unsure how long it would take him to get cleared.

I had believed that FBI agent's words. He was so convincing, but Rocky had been right. Renza was arrested, too. She was going to hate me for the rest of her life. I had never felt so low in my life, ever. I was so humiliated.

Now that the banks were no longer a secret, there was nothing at all keeping me tied to Dino anymore. I no longer felt obligated to talk to him; however, I did feel badly. He may have been a real jerk to me, but at the end of the day I caused him a lot of pain. I should know better than anyone that sometimes you are not yourself when you have a broken heart. I didn't blame him fully; I was to blame, too, that Rocky's career was ruined.

Renza was not proud of herself and would have taken it all back if she could, I know that. Sometimes I'd want to tell her that I knew she meant well and that I could see in her eyes and hear in her voice her regret, but I didn't even want to bring it up to her. I think she just wanted to forget everything she had done; it was too much for her to live with.

Renza made some bad choices, but she was far from a bad person. I remember back one year at Easter time, she found out that my mom didn't have much money to get my siblings baskets and chocolates, so she scrounged up everything she had and brought it to my mom. It was almost one hundred dollars. No matter what, that woman has a good heart and would always help others if she could. It was her little way of making up for her wrongdoings, and her efforts don't go unnoticed.

Rocky decided to rent a car. He was really not supposed to, but he was all alone and just needed to come home for a bit, and he wanted to spend time with his dad. I did not go with him to spend time with Dom because I was too embarrassed.

The next morning he called me and then he came and picked me up. It felt amazing to finally see him after so long. We hugged each other so tight and he had this huge, excited smile that he couldn't wipe off of his face. I had caused all of this to happen in his life, and he still loved me so much.

The next morning we met my papa for breakfast, and then it was goodbye. He had to get back to Fort Jackson by Monday morning. I could see that he didn't want to leave me; it was hard for the both of us.

A couple of weeks later, Rocky was cleared out of Fort Jackson and transported to the local county jail in Pennsylvania. My papa bailed him out all on his own. Nobody asked him to, but we were grateful. Rocky paid him back that very night. Rocky made bad choices before he left for the service, but he went overseas into harm's way to fight for this country of ours and was without a weapon over there for some time; he didn't deserve any of that!

My papa never felt sorry for anyone easily, but anyone with a heart knew that Rocky was dealt a dirty hand. My Grandfather had his back and wanted to help him in any way that he could. Before we knew it, my grandfather had all sorts of letters written from others that didn't like what happened to Rocky either—lawyers, Senators, business owners. Rocky's sergeants and other soldiers that he served with all wrote letters for him too. The letters stated how much of an asset Rocky was to them, and all of the hard work he had done, the instances where Rocky went above and beyond and where he would take it upon himself to do things to help out when not even asked.

All of these letters had a purpose, which was to help Rocky get back into the army. We were very hopeful, especially with so many other voices willing to speak for him.

◆

Rocky and I stayed at a motel for a little while, and then we moved in with Dom after we noticed that he was becoming forgetful. Dom's mind seemed like it was going. He would complain that we ate all of the food in the house, and then we would open the fridge and cupboards up to show him that they were stocked. He forgot how to lock and unlock the door. Rocky's Uncle Corey was Dom's power of attorney. He would only give him so much money at a time, and Dom would call him for more money, not remembering whether he had spent it or put it away. He was in the early stages of Alzheimer's.

As the days passed, I started becoming tired all of the time and nauseous. For a little while before that began, I had thoughts that I might be pregnant, although deep down I told myself that I wasn't. I finally went and bought a test.

I waited until the next morning to take the test, because I knew that morning urine was the best urine to take it with. When the next morning came, I went into the bathroom to take it. Rocky came in, too, and stood right in front of the test blocking my view.

"We're pregnant!"

I grabbed the test. It was a faint line, but it was definitely there. We hugged and laughed. Rocky was out his mind, crazy-happy. Rocky walked out of the bathroom and I looked into the mirror at myself and realized something.

"Oh no…" I said quietly while looking at myself in the mirror. "This baby might be Dino's."

My happiness instantly became sadness. I couldn't put Rocky through any more. I went to the bed and lay down for a bit. I had to stop thinking about the paternity for a couple of minutes. I just wanted to think about my baby. Wow, I was really excited for this! I kept looking at my stomach, and putting my hands on it. I loved this peanut already!

I wanted to tell the world the news, but I had to wait. After a few minutes, Rocky came into the room. He was so excited that he was going to be a dad. He had always wanted a family and always wanted children. He was on cloud nine. He told me that he left a phone book on the kitchen table so we could look up local baby doctors. He was totally on top of this! It was so attractive to see him so into this.

CHAPTER 30

The next time Dino called me he was back in Louisiana, and I was at my mom's house visiting. I didn't realize until that phone call that he had gone back there. He said that he went to get his family back, but it didn't work out. He and his wife got back together for a few days but it didn't last. That made me sad. I was rooting for his daughter to have her mom and dad together again.

"You are my last chance for happiness," he kept repeating.

Dino sounded very quiet and sad when he spoke.

"Dino, I want you to fix things with your family. I don't want to hear how sad you are. It makes me sad. You will always hold a special place in my heart, but I have to be honest with myself and with everyone else now. Things shouldn't have gone this far between you and me. You abused and tortured me, lied, and ruined Rocky's army career for him."

"Alright, Rose, I get it...... I will always love you."

And he hung up.

In that moment, I felt so sorry for him. I have caused sadness all over. I hoped Dino was okay, and I hoped he, Rita and their daughter could become a family again. Most of all, I hoped that he would get some help. He needed a therapist; he needed some talking to.

The next day was a day that I would never forget for the rest of my life, although I wish I could wipe it away from my memory. I was at work and there was a snow storm. I ran out to warm up my car and scrape the ice off the windshield. It was so cold out and there were at least ten people outside also trying to scrape ice off of their vehicles. It was just insane.

At 9:15 p.m. I was finally on my way home after almost 30 minutes of freezing my butt off outside. When I arrived home, I walked in and Dom had dinner waiting for me. He was so good to me, and so excited for the baby. After everything that I had put this family through, he still loved me as his daughter. I didn't deserve it, really.

Rocky had the bed made for me. He had the DVD player all set to watch one of my favorite shows, The King of Queens, and he had some popcorn made. They were really too good to me, considering everything.

Dom was watching TV in his recliner in the living room, and Rocky and I were sitting up in bed eating popcorn, talking, laughing and having a great time. I started paying more attention to the TV because one of my favorite episodes was playing.

Dom came in the room and said something to Rocky, but I wasn't paying much attention. I wasn't sure what he said, but Rocky left the room and walked out into the hallway. I thought he was probably helping Dom with something. I continued watching my show.

I was so into my show, but all of a sudden, I heard something and I looked and there was Rocky lying on the floor in the hallway, not saying anything. I flew up out of the bed as Dom walked over and stood over Rocky. As I bolted toward them, Dom yelled to me.

"STAY BACK! GET IN THE ROOM!"

"WHAT HAPPENED?" I yelled back.

No one was answering me. I froze, panicking because I knew something bad just happened, but I didn't know what. All sorts of thoughts began to run through my mind. I knew it was serious enough that I needed to call the police, but my phone was dead and Rocky's was probably in his pocket; I didn't see it anywhere.

"Call the police!" Rocky began to yell.

"Why! Why! What's happening?" I screamed back.

The hallway made an L shape, and the room was at the end of the "L," so the way that Rocky was lying I could only see his head and shoulders but not the rest of him.

"WHY IS HE ON THE FLOOR?" I screamed.

I needed to call cops but I had no cell phone to use and I couldn't go into the kitchen, so going out the window to use a neighbors phone to call the police was my only option. Frantically as I was opening the window to climb out, Rocky called out to me as he finally got up.

"No! Dino is out there! Get away from the window! He's got a gun!"

Now Rocky had gotten up, and he and Dom came and grabbed me on each side and hid me in the hall closet. Then Dom went and grabbed the house phone on the wall and stretched it as far as it would go so I could use it from inside the closet. Dom dialed 911 before handing me the phone and I told them what was going on.

The police arrived within minutes. They asked Rocky what happened.

"I was watching TV with my girlfriend, and my dad came to the room and said someone was at the door for me. When I walked to the door, I knew it was Dino and I looked up at the ceiling and sighed because I knew it wasn't going to be good. When I looked back at him before I went to open the glass door I saw him reach into the inside of his coat pocket, and I just knew what he had in there. He pulled out a gun, pointed it at me and pulled the trigger. I jumped out of the way and laid on the floor."

It was a nightmare! But I thought Dino was in Louisiana—how could it be him? The cop then asked Rocky what he was wearing, and Rocky said that he had on a black jacket, jeans and a hat. Instantly, by the description Rocky had given, I knew it was him. He was back! How did he figure out where we lived? I just wanted the cops to find him, because I would not feel safe until he was caught.

I decided to try to call Dino so that maybe I could get his location. I called him over and over and over again, but no answer. The cops went to his in-laws to see if he was hiding there, because his car was registered to their address. I knew he wouldn't go there.

Dom was a trooper. In the midst of all this madness, he threw a pizza in the oven and started microwaving other food. He was trying to get me to eat but I just couldn't.

About an hour after searching for Dino, I heard a call come though the radio that belonged to one of the police men.

"It's him. What do we do now?" the person over the phone asked.

I thought to myself, *what do you mean what do we do now?* After a few minutes, I thought it was odd that no one was coming to talk to me and let me know what was going on. I walked over to them with my question.

"Have you found Dino yet?"

They all looked at each other, and then one police officer came forward to talk to me.

"Why don't you go have a seat at the table?"

I knew it must have been bad. What if Dino hurt my family? I had called them earlier and told them all to lock their doors because he was back and armed. I sat down as the officers all came and stood around the table, looking at me in sorrow.

"I am very sorry to tell you this, but Dino is now deceased," officer Hank said to me.

I stood up, and sat down, and then stood up and sat down again, crying and at the same time, not believing it. They said he took his own life. I just cried and wanted to actually see him because he just couldn't be dead. I looked down at my stomach and was overcome with the freakiest feeling that I might be carrying a dead man's baby.

Rocky held me.

"I know you loved him, Rose. I know you did. It's going to be okay, I promise you."

Dom was gently rubbing my back. I was numb. I asked the officers to describe to me the tattoos on the body, because I did not believe that it was Dino. They were able to describe tattoos that I knew Dino had, including the last one, "Rose," on his forearm. The pain I was feeling was beyond words. Dino was really gone. I felt to blame. I was so furious with the guy just 10 minutes before this and now I was feeling so very sorry for him.

Rocky was so lucky to be alive, so as badly as I was hurting in that moment, I was also relieved, very grateful and thanking God that Rocky hadn't been taken from me.

The Policemen had called a lady to come and sit with me for a couple of hours. She was very sweet; she was a counselor for situations like this. I couldn't sleep there—I was too shaken up and freaked out. I didn't want to leave Dom, but he said he was fine. I needed to go and sleep at my grandparents' house.

Rocky didn't want to leave my side, so he wanted to come with me. I really needed Rocky to stay with me. I wanted Dom to come with us, too, but he wouldn't come. Everyone was so worried about me, but I wasn't the one who was shot at. Rocky had told me, "I was overseas. I'm used to stuff like this, I'm fine." He's so modest, one of the things I love most about him

Dom hugged me, told me he loved me, and said he was going to have a beer and watch some more TV. He said he was full from eating so much. He was a tough man. I still felt bad to leave him there, but he didn't seem phased. I knew that he was just happy that his son was okay.

We got to my grandparents, and Rocky and I made up the couch for us to sleep on. My grandparents sat up with us for an hour or so. When they went to bed, I told Rocky that I was nervous because there might be a chance that the baby was Dino's.

"I know," he said.

"You do?"

"Yes, Rose. You think I didn't realize that myself? But I have a good feeling about the baby and I am not worried, that's why it doesn't bother me. My good feelings are usually right, but even if the baby doesn't turn out to be biologically mine, I'll still be his or her father."

I loved this man more than words could ever explain. I was truly lucky. He deserved so much better than me.

◆

I spoke to Dino's good friend's mother the next day. He took his life at her house in front of her son, his good friend. I went over there to talk with her.

When I walked in, they tried to cover up where he did it the best they could. They used a blanket to cover the floor so I didn't have to see much, but his blood was on the walls too. On a table next to the spot, they had a candle burning with a picture of him and me next to it. The picture was an old one from when I was fifteen. He was holding that picture and rosary beads when he left this world. Dino was praying to God for forgiveness for what he did to Rocky right before he shot himself.

The emotional pain was almost unbearable. I kept thinking about his little girl and how she no longer had a dad here, and it was all my fault. I didn't stay long. I couldn't.

CHAPTER 31

A couple of days passed and the sadness didn't really subside much. By now, I finally knew all about morning sickness. I didn't actually throw up, but I got so nauseated to the point where I felt like I needed to badly, and I'd just lie down or sit still until it went away. I had to keep reminding myself that I was really going to be a mom. It still felt like a dream. I just wished that I knew for sure who the father was.

◆

Dino's wake and funeral were held a few days later. I was very nervous, but I had to attend. I didn't know if people would blame me, or want me to leave, but I felt it was something I needed to do.

When I arrived, Rita and I hugged and cried, and I wrapped my arms around his little girl. Rita and I never had nice words with each other once. We never, ever got along, but when hugging her I felt so close to her and felt so sorry for her. I had no more angry feelings toward her; I almost felt like I cared about her. It was like we had a bond in that moment. Dino's daughter had his face—it was so unbelievable to me. Dino's father came over to talk to me.

"Rose, this life just wasn't for him. He talked about taking his own life for a long time. He was sick and couldn't control it," he told me.

His uncles came over and apologized for what happened. They said they would like to reach out to Rocky's family and tell them how sorry they were for what happened. I got to meet Dino's mother and brother for the first time, and they were very kind to me. His grandmothers were sweet as well, and his friends.

I thought when I got there that I would get heat, but I got love instead. I did receive some heat from people who weren't really close to him. They attacked me through Myspace messages—kind of like when somebody dies and everybody wants to be their best friend because they want attention or just wished they had given the person who passed more attention when they were alive, so they try to give it to them after they're gone.

Dino's close family and closest friends were very good to me. His dad said the only ones who would be mad at me were the ones who weren't as close with him, the ones who didn't know what he was like, the ones that didn't know that this life did not make him happy.

"I wondered when you would get out," his dad said to me. "I saw your black eyes and I knew they weren't from running into a door or whatever you said it was from. You were smart to get out when you did."

Just because I chose Rocky over Dino did not mean that I didn't care for Dino, because I did. I only wished he could still be here on this earth, happy, with his daughter and his daughter's mom, and with no mental issues. I feel safer now, though. I am not afraid of him anymore. He can't hurt me now. I just wish that I could have done something to help him, something to save his mind.

I thought back to what might have happened. If I had heard Dom tell Rocky that someone was at the door for him, I might have wondered who it was and I would have gotten up to see, and if that had happened, I don't think I'd still be alive.

I thanked God for not letting me hear when Dom told Rocky someone was there to see him. Dino used to say he was going to kill me and then take his own life, and I am as certain as my eyes are brown that if he had seen me, he would have done just that. Rocky was not angry with Dino, he forgave him. Rocky actually wrote Dino a beautifully touching letter that my mother held onto for safe keeping:

Dino,

I don't know if you did what you did when you shot at me out of anger or if you planned it, but I want you to know that I forgive you. I forgive you for shooting at me. Rose is so upset over what happened and she still can't believe you're gone. I wish that day never happened. Don't worry about the baby. Whether it's mine or yours, I'm going to take good care of it and make sure that he or she never goes without.

Rocky

CHAPTER 32

Three months had passed and I was still having an awful time coping with what happened. I moved back in with my grandparents. I couldn't sleep in a bedroom, I could only sleep in a living room. The nighttime scared me. I could not shower alone—when I'd get in the shower, I'd make one of my sisters or Rocky come and sit on the toilet until I was done. When I would finally fall asleep, the smell of beer and cigarettes would wake me up in the middle of the night. Dino often used to smell like that, and I often wondered if it was him visiting me.

I didn't know when I would be okay again, but a wonderful, supportive family and sweet Rocky definitely helped. I was so angry with Dino even though he was gone, because my life was turned upside down the night that he did what he did. I felt like I'd be scared forever. I just wanted to cope with everything and feel better, but it seemed as if it would never happen.

There's some good news regarding my mother. She got rid of her awful boyfriend, Sparky. Sparky doesn't have anything to do with my little brother anymore but my brother will be okay as he has all of us. My mom started seeing a man named Lorenzo. She's known him since they were little, and his parents were friends with my grandparents. Lorenzo and my mother got engaged and he treats my little brother like he is his own!

On another note—a very exciting note— Rocky and I found out that we would be welcoming a little girl, and we were so thrilled! One afternoon, Dino's mom called me and was telling me about a dream that she had. She said that I was standing in front of Dino's casket in a black dress with a big baby bump and Dino's ghost was standing beside me crying while looking at my stomach as if he knew the baby wasn't his. She said she felt like her dream was a sign that he baby was not Dino's. She said she'd love that baby anyway. She was so kind to me, and my heart hurt for her because Dino was the second son that she had to burry.

If this whole experience taught me anything, it was that life isn't always fair, people are going to make mistakes, and do not ever think you are allowed to intentionally hurt someone or play the karma card, because it will backfire in your face. It taught me that being deceitful and dishonest to others is not a quality that I wanted within myself. I would rather get hurt and forgive than purposely try to hurt anybody to make myself feel better. That doesn't work.

Being good to people makes you feel good. Making someone smile makes you feel good. Making someone upset never once truly felt good in my heart, even though I kept claiming that it did.

I hadn't been honest with myself, and I paid for it. God punished me, I believe. Granted, I brought everything on myself. I learned that when it comes to the female gender, being madly in love and having a broken heart doesn't mix well; in my case, it created smoke and deceitful actions create the fire. *Sow the wind, reap the whirlwind.* I did just that, and I reaped every consequence of my actions.

◆

A lot happened in the six years that followed. I welcomed a beautiful 7 pound 5 ounce baby girl into the world. She came six days late, and I was scared when I went into labor, but my whole family was at that hospital with me, and then I saw her for the first time and I was madly in love with her.

Rocky was sentenced to some prison time and then shock camp. Shock camp is almost like basic training but it is for inmates. They have to get accepted into the program and once completed, the inmates get released on parole. He had also been granted youthful offender status and was home nine months later after Shock camp.

A little over one year after Rocky came home, we welcomed another baby, a wonderful 5 pound 13 ounce baby boy. Shortly after our son was born, we lost Dom. It was a very hard, painful time. I will always treasure the wonderful memories that I have of him. I'll remember how much his eyes lit up when his little granddaughter came into the room, and the way he'd smile while talking about one of his kids. He loved all of his kids so much.

My son was too little to take him into hospice, so Dom never got to hold him, but he loved him before he was even born and the way that he talks about his Papa D today, you wouldn't know that he had never met him.

Rocky and I got married in October of 2010, on our 5-year anniversary of getting together! We experienced some major ups and downs that first year of marriage. Sometimes I did not know how we would make it through as a couple. Everything that we went through during our relationship was enough to tear any couple apart. We chose to stay together, but all that happened took a toll on us as a couple.

We started going to church and reading our bibles, and we fought through. Our relationship now is solid and stronger than ever, and we pray that it remains that way. We put our marriage first before anything. Our relationship survived with a lot of patience and understanding, and last but not least, with the power of prayer.

God is good, but his lessons are tough. I always knew deep down no matter what we were going through that I would marry Rocky. I was ready to marry him when I was seventeen!

Twenty-two months after our son was born, we had another daughter, the missing piece to our puzzle, the one who completed our little family, a 6 pound 4 ounce sweet baby girl. On Valentine's Day of 2012, we received the results in the mail of the paternity test that we finally decided to get done when she was 3 years old.

That was a joyous day, finding out that we no longer had to wonder or be nervous about the truth, because we finally knew that Rocky was her biological dad. Rocky played a little prank on me while he was reading it. He quickly opened it up and his face became sad while reading it and I thought, *Oh, no! Oh, no!* And then he yelled, "She's mine!!!" He actually had already read it with my grandma and stuck it back in the envelope as I was pulling in from school, so he already knew before we opened it together.

Realistically, Dino did not have a good chance because of the timeline and the date that the doctor estimated that I conceived; however, it was still a possibility. Another reason that it was unlikely that Dino was the father was because it had taken three years to conceive his daughter, and after she was born, he and his daughter's mother tried for years, the remainder of their relationship, to have another baby but were unsuccessful. They were hoping for a son. His dad and grandma said he smoked way too much marijuana and that was why he had such a hard time having a baby.

The last reason that it was unlikely that it was Dino's baby was because Rocky came home and boom, I was pregnant less than two months later.

There were only two reasons why I thought Dino might have fathered the baby. The first reason was because I've always heard that "death brings new life," and I thought since he died that it was God leaving a piece of Dino here.

The next reason that also had made me think that Dino was the father had happened one month before I gave birth to my daughter. I was sitting in the computer room at my grandparents, hormonal, emotional and crying a little over everything. My phone beeped. It was a text message. It read "*I miss U 2*" and it was from my mom's cell phone number. I texted back a question mark and I got another text that read "*I love you.*" I could feel that something was odd in that moment or maybe my mom was texting the wrong person but I didn't think it was her because she doesn't type that way. I wrote back asking, "Who is this"? My Phone went off again and it read, "Its Dino" — at that point, I called my mom's phone.

"What is going on, are you texting me that? Who is using your phone?"

"Texting you what?"

I read the messages to her.

"It's just me and your little brother here! I didn't send that, and I know my three-year-old didn't…are you sure Rose?"

I hung up on her because I got another message and this time it said "*I'm so sorry I love you.,, so much and I am so. so sorry for everything that. I did to you and I'm so sorry to Rocky. Please forgive me take. care of the baby. I LOVE U!*"

That is what it said, with all the crazy punctuation. Either this was Dino contacting me or someone was playing an evil prank on me.

My mother came over to see the text messages that came from her phone number, and she was in disbelief. I turned my phone off and I took the battery out that night so nothing would happen to that phone and I could save those text messages. I activated a new phone the next day.

I wanted to show Dino's dad the messages when he stopped over, but when I turned my phone on to show him the next day, they were gone! Only those four text messages were gone! Was I spoofed by some awful, evil person or was it really him? I guess I'll never know.

I thought the text saying "take care of the baby" was a sign from him that it was his baby, although it did say "the baby" instead of "my baby," so I probably shouldn't have taken it that way. At the time of receiving that, I wasn't thinking any clear thoughts.

The part that gets me is that Dino had just started learning to text a month or two before he passed away, and he hated texting. His text messages were always a bit messy with periods and commas in random places, just like the text messages I received that night. I felt like if someone was trying to do something to me like spoof my phone, they would have written some not-so-nice things, instead of what the messages said, but again— I will never know where they came from.

Instead of Dino's death becoming easier to accept with time, it became harder to deal with and I lost contact with Dino's entire family. I felt ashamed as time went on, and anyone he knew was just a sore reminder of him for me. It hurt too much. I was sure that I was just as sore a reminder for them, but they still loved me.

I had been through too much and I needed to get away from anything that reminded me of him in order for me to get better. I hated feeling like I was the reason that someone wasn't on this earth anymore. I hoped things would change in the future, because his family are good people and I will always love them, despite what they may think. I think of them often, especially Dino's daughter, even though she might not think that I do. I felt truly sorry about anyone that I had hurt.

Now, Rocky and I both have decent jobs. He is in the laborers union and I went to school for Personal Lines/Property and Casualty insurance.

We have three wonderful children and are working toward buying our first home.

Renza did five years in a correctional facility. Brayden and I received full immunity. Needless to say, Renza and I hardly spoke while she was away, not because of her, though, but because of me. I felt so badly that I was the reason she was in there. She sent me cards for holidays and she would write that she was not mad at me, but I was mad at me. She would say that she did what she did and told me when things are done in the dark, God brings them to light.

Sometimes when wanting to describe something so perfectly regarding what you see or what you may feel, well, sometimes words just fail. What you see and know sometimes can't be put into words, only into thoughts. The words are hard to find that describe the regret that I could see that Renza carried around with her, the look in her face, the sound of her voice, her effort in turning her relationship with God around – everything about her screamed that she was sorry. Sometimes to see the way that someone truly feels, you have to look past words and intently hear their behavior instead. I'm certain that if time rewound itself, Renza would never have even mentioned a bank. There is nothing more beautiful than redemption. I used to think that nobody could change, and Renza changed that way of thinking for me.

When Renza went before her parole board, she was expecting not to make parole because we were told in most cases you don't make it the first try even though she had never been in trouble before in her life. When she was asked why she deserved to get out on a parole, her response was this:

> "Weather I deserve to be released is questionable. I made innocent people fear me. Even though I didn't use a weapon, they were still scared. I knew that I wasn't going to hurt them, but they didn't know that I wasn't going to hurt them. I can't make anyone understand how sorry that I am, but I am so, so sorry to the tellers and also to their families."

That was on a Friday and then on the following Tuesday she found out that she had made parole. The Correctional officers were so happy for her, and we were all so happy back at home for her. She was liked by everyone there and they were going to miss her, but I finally felt a sense of relief knowing that she was coming home.

More than anything though, I'm disappointed in the way that Rocky was treated. At the end of the day, he is a Veteran and he fought for our country. He risked his life every day that he was overseas for us. Rocky committed a crime, absolutely, but this wasn't your typical situation. The Army meant so much to him, it was who he was, who he still is. He loves his country and it's a shame that anyone let the loss of his Army career happen to him after everything was said and done, especially after the FBI guaranteed he would remain in the military.

The entire situation is sad, but nothing is worse than an American Soldier being treated so poorly. However, had none of it ever happened, we wouldn't have had our children when we did because Rocky would have still been in Iraq when our first little girl was conceived. Maybe we would still have had a family and a life together if none of what we went through ever happened, but maybe not. We will never know.

Maybe Rocky would have never made it home; maybe we would have lost him over there. We don't know why things happen the way they do, but I have to believe that things just happen the way that they are supposed to. There was beauty that came out of the ugliness. Things surely have a funny way of working out, and there is a lesson to be learned—always.